Diet recommendations for Hypertension

Please check these recommendations always with a nutrition consultant, therapist, doctor or dietician. The recipes and the list of ingredients are supporting the conventional medical therapy.
The calorie disclosures of fresh ingredients (fruit and vegetables) vary according to quality and time of harvest. The contents were checked by a dietician and a nutrition consultant for the Traditional Chinese Medicine (TCM).

Author:
©2019 Josef Miligui
www.ebns.at

AF200031

Source:
The lists are created from the EBNS database for nutritional counseling. The database is used by dietitians, therapists and doctors for advising the patient / client.

Literature:
The specialist literature and the training documents of the German and Austrian dietary and traditional Chinese medicine serve as a knowledge base. We have used the documents as a basis of knowledge, adapted it to our experience and completed them.
http://di-book.com

Production and publishing:
BoD – Books on Demand, Norderstedt
ISBN: 9783746043920

Diet recommendations for DIETETICS - Metabolism - Heart and circulation - Hypertension

1   Treatment strategy

Dairy foods, low-fat diet, weight reduction, less salt.
Omega-3 fatty acids help reduce blood pressure.
Vitamin D deficiency balance with fish (cod liver oil, mackerel, salmon or herring), mushrooms, beef liver, Emmental, butter, organic eggs, avocados.
Approximately 80% to 90% of our most important vitamin D reserves are developed by the sun from the body itself. Even 5 to 15 minutes a day are enough to stimulate the body's vitamin D production.

2   Avoid

If you are overweight, the consumption of fats should be restricted.
Caution especially with hidden fats in sausage and cheese, cakes and pastries, sweets and nuts.
Avoid alcohol and nicotine.
Highly salted food.

3 Breakfast

4 Snack

5 Lunch

6   Afternoon

7   Dinner

8   Any time

9 Recipes

(rec.) = You can use more.
(little) = You should use less than specified
(no) omit.

9.1 Apple - banana cream

Regulates gastrointestinal function, provides vitamin C, cholesterol lowering, reduces inflammation, diuretic, improves blood circulation.
Cooking time approx. 15 min
4 portions to 206,25g. / 110kcal. - (carb:94% / prot:6%)
100g.=53,45kcal. / protein 0,84g. fat:0,51g.
µg. - Ph:0,75 Na:0,12 Ka:9,5 Mg:0,68 Ca:0,56 Fe:0,03 Zn:0,01 Col.:0 Hsr.:0,8

Quantity of ingredients:
Apple (sour) 7/8 lbs / 400g. (yes)
Water 3/4 cup - 6 oz / 200g. (yes)
Orange peel 1/4 piece / 5g. (yes)
Lemon peel 1/2 piece / 2g. (yes)
Sugar brown 2 teaspoons / 6g. (little)
Cinnamon sticks 1 piece / 0g. (yes)
Banana 1 piece / 150g. (yes)
Acerola fruit nectar or powder 1 teaspoon / 2g. (little)
Orange juice 1/2 piece / 50g. (little)
Lemon juice 1 table spoon / 10g. (yes)

Cooking instructions:
Cut the apple into fine slices, bring water to boil and add the apple slices, orange- and lemon peel, sugar and cinnamon and simmer about 7 minutes. The apples should be almost soft. Remove acerola and the cinnamon stick. Mix the apple, the banana, the orange juice and the lemon juice.

9.2 Asparagus and herb ragout

Diuretic, improves blood circulation, prevents cancer, dissolves stagnation, promotes weight loss. Good to fight immunodeficiency, loss of appetite, flatulence, high blood pressure, depressions, diabetes, diarrhea, stimulates liver function.
Cooking time approx. 30 min
Allergens: GL

4 portions to 465,5g. / 168kcal. - (carb:78% / prot:22%)
100g.=36,14kcal. / protein 7,54g. fat:4,09g.
µg. - Ph:2,55 Na:0,54 Ka:11,94 Mg:2,69 Ca:9,45 Fe:0,06 Zn:0,02 Col.:0 Hsr.:1,09

Quantity of ingredients:
Basic recipe for a vegetable soup (nutritious) 2 cups / 500g. (yes)
Lemon peel 1/2 piece / 3g. (yes)
Coriander 1/4 teaspoon / 1g. (yes)
Nutmeg 1 pinch / 0,3g. (yes)
Asparagus (green or white) 1,8 lbs / 800g. (yes)
Parsley 1 Bunch / 125g. (yes)
Crème fraiche cheese 2 table spoons / 30g. (little)
Lemon juice 1 teaspoon / 3g. (yes)
Potato 7/8 lbs / 400g. (yes)

Cooking instructions:
Cook potatoes with plenty of salted water about 20 min. until soft.
Heat the vegetable stock with lemon zest, coriander and nutmeg till it
boil. Cook the peeled and sliced asparagus in it.
Drain asparagus in a sieve. Collect the cooking liquid.
In the blender mix 200 g of cooked asparagus (the lower ends), cooking
liquid and parsley to a smooth sauce. Beat the sauce with crème
fraîche until smooth. Add asparagus and heat again and season with
lemon juice, salt and pepper. Serve with the potatoes.

9.3   Banana Soymilk

Good to fight loss of appetite, oral mucosa inflammation. Strengthens
body energy, promotes stomach-spleen harmony, promotes digestion,
regulates gastrointestinal function. Relieves pain, detoxifying,
bactericide.
Cooking time approx. 5 min
Allergens: E
2 portions to 263g. / 126kcal. - (carb:60% / prot:40%)
100g.=47,72kcal. / protein 7,49g. fat:4,13g.
µg. - Ph:10,97 Na:125,56 Ka:55,04 Mg:6,65 Ca:4,89 Fe:0,2 Zn:0,11 Col.:0 Hsr.:16,84

Quantity of ingredients:
Banana 1 piece / 120g. (yes)
Soybean milk 1 1/2 cups / 400g. (yes)
Honey 1 teaspoon / 3g. (little)
Cinnamon ground 1 pinch / 1g. (yes)
Acerola fruit nectar or powder 1 teaspoon / 2g. (little)

Cooking instructions:
Cut the banana into pieces, puree them with soy milk, acerola, honey and cinnamon with the mixing stick.

9.4   Barley and vegetable soup

Supports urination, detoxifying, promotes spleen and liver, reduces blood pressure, strengthens immune system, prevents cancer, reduces radiation damage, promotes digestion, helps to digest fat, harmonizes metabolism.
Cooking time approx. 2 hours
Allergens: AGL
3 portions to 304g. / 281kcal. - (carb:73% / prot:27%)
100g.=92,54kcal. / protein 11,93g. fat:5,74g.
µg. - Ph:9,75 Na:1,36 Ka:21,85 Mg:3,27 Ca:3,09 Fe:0,14 Zn:0,08 Col.:0,09 Hsr.:9,52

Quantity of ingredients:
Barley 1 cup / 120g. (yes)
Shiitake, dried 1/8 oz / 4g. (yes)
Onion (shallot) 1 piece / 20g. (yes)
Cumin (Caraway seed) 1 knife tip / 0,5g. (yes)
Sunflower oil 1 table spoon / 10g. (yes)
Water 1 cup / 250g. (yes)
Celery sticks 2 branches / 20g. (yes)
Peas, green 5/8 lbs - 8oz / 250g. (yes)
Tomato 1 piece / 50g. (yes)
Carrot 2 pieces / 150g. (yes)
French beans 1 handful / 30g. (yes)
Salt 1 pinch / 1g. (little)
Pepper (ground) 1 pinch / 0,5g. ()
Parsley 1 teaspoon / 3g. (yes)
Butter organic 1 teaspoon / 3g. (little)

Cooking instructions:
Soak the barley in the evening for the next day. Soak the mushrooms separately at the next day. Brown onion and cumin in oil, then boil with water. Add the chopped vegetables, some salt, the barley and the shiitake mushrooms and cook everything to a thick soup. At the end, season with pepper, parsley and a little butter.

9.5 Barley mash with berries

Diuretic, forcing spleen, supports urination, laxative, strengthens kidney, promotes digestion, detoxifying, promotes perspiration, reduces blood lipids, stimulates, dissolves stagnation.
Cooking time approx. 2 hours
Allergens: A
5 portions to 318,6g. / 113kcal. - (carb:82% / prot:18%)
100g.=35,34kcal. / protein 4,01g. fat:0,78g.
µg. - Ph:1,47 Na:0,11 Ka:2,69 Mg:0,63 Ca:0,55 Fe:0,02 Zn:0,01 Col.:0 Hsr.:0,48

Quantity of ingredients:
Water 10 cups / 1200g. (yes)
Barley 1 cup / 120g. (yes)
Ginger fresh 2 slices / 2g. (yes)
Cardamom 3 capsules / 1g. (yes)
Salt 1 pinch / 1g. (little)
Raspberry 5/8 lbs - 8oz / 250g. (yes)
Cocoa 1 pinch / 1g. (rec.)
Barley malt 1 table spoon / 15g. (yes)
Lemon Balm (fresh) 2-4 leaves / 3g. (yes)

Cooking instructions:
Boil the barley with water, ginger and cardamom pods in a large saucepan. Close pot with a lid and cook over low heat for about 2 hours.

For 2 servings of cooked barley porridge, place about 2 ladles in a bowl. Stir with sunflower seeds, malt, cocoa powder and a pinch of salt. Stir fresh berries into the porridge and serve sprinkled with fresh mint or lemon balm.
Tip: The pre-cooked barley porridge (without fruit) can be stored well in the refrigerator and used for sweet or savory dishes, e.g. with stewed vegetables or fruit seasoned compote.

9.6 Barley mash with steamed pear

Promotes digestion, supports urination, promotes spleen, diuretic, forcing spleen, relaxes, promotes perspiration.
Cooking time approx. 25 min
Allergens: A
5 portions to 305,8g. / 114kcal. - (carb:86% / prot:14%)
100g.=37,21kcal. / protein 3,26g. fat:0,72g.
µg. - Ph:1,16 Na:0,11 Ka:2,09 Mg:0,44 Ca:0,33 Fe:0,01 Zn:0,01 Col.:0 Hsr.:0,42

Quantity of ingredients:
Water 10 cups / 1200g. (yes)
Barley 1 cup / 120g. (yes)
Ginger fresh 2 slices / 2g. (yes)
Cardamom 3 capsules / 1g. (yes)
Salt 1 pinch / 1g. (little)
Pear 1 piece / 200g. (yes)
Sugar cane sugar 1/2 teaspoon / 5g. (little)

Cooking instructions:
Grind coarse the barley and roast it dry. Add hot water, add ginger and cardamom and let it swell to a pulp in low heat. Peel and dice the pear and boil for 10 minutes with a little water. At the end, add the stewed pear, a little butter and sweetener.

Variant: If you want to go fast, you can use barley flakes instead of shot.

9.7 Basic recipe for a chicken broth worming

Strengthens blood, strengthens bone marrow, reduces blood pressure, strengthens immune system, prevents cancer, reduces radiation damage, promotes sweating, dissolves stagnation, good to fight loss of appetite, flatulence.
Cooking time approx. 2-3 hours
Allergens: L
9 portions to 244,89g. / 90kcal. - (carb:10% / prot:90%)
100g.=36,66kcal. / protein 15,68g. fat:11,56g.
µg. - Ph:0,86 Na:0,59 Ka:1,87 Mg:0,13 Ca:0,38 Fe:0,01 Zn:0 Col.:0,25 Hsr.:0,92

Quantity of ingredients:
Chicken meat 1/2 piece / 600g. (yes)
Carrot 2 pieces / 150g. (yes)
Leek 1 stick / 45g. (yes)
Celery root 1 piece / 500g. (yes)
Ginger fresh 2 slices / 2g. (yes)
Fenugreek (Trigonella foenum-graecum) 1 teaspoon / 2g. (yes)
Juniper berry 1 teaspoon / 3g. (yes)
Bay leaf 3 pieces / 2g. (yes)
Water 4 cup / 900g. (yes)

Cooking instructions:
Remove chicken parts from fat. Place chicken pieces in a saucepan with hot water and heat till it boils briefly, skimming any resulting foam. Add coarsely chopped vegetables and all spices and cook over medium

heat for 2 to 3 hours. Strain the finished soup. Throw away vegetables and bones.

Tip: If you want to use the meat as a soup insert, take out after 45 minutes and return only the bones in the soup.

Refrigerate for later use.

9.8   Basic recipe for a fish broth

Strengthens the kidneys, promotes watering, reduces blood pressure, strengthens immune system, prevents cancer, reduces radiation damage. Low in cholesterol and protein rich. Improves blood circulation, stimulates appetite.

Cooking time approx. 40 min

Allergens: DLO

5 portions to 243,8g. / 128kcal. - (carb:34% / prot:66%)
100g.=52,34kcal. / protein 9,81g. fat:5,2g.
µg. - Ph:14,91 Na:7,09 Ka:31,5 Mg:2,39 Ca:4,63 Fe:0,11 Zn:0,02 Col.:0,01 Hsr.:11,94

Quantity of ingredients:
Fish pieces mixed (fresh water) 3/4 lbs / 300g. (yes)
Celery root 1/4 lbs - 4oz / 120g. (yes)
Leek 2 inches / 10g. (yes)
Carrot 2 pieces / 150g. (yes)
White wine 1/2 cup / 125g. (little)
Lemon 1/2 piece / 50g. (yes)
Bay leaf 2 leaves / 2g. (yes)
Peppercorns 3 pieces / 2g. (yes)
Olive oil 1 table spoon / 10g. (yes)
Water 2 cup / 450g. (yes)

Cooking instructions:
Fry celery, chopped carrots and leeks in olive oil, add bay leaf and peppercorns, add pieces of fish and sauté briefly. Add water, add little white wine or lemon. Simmer gently for 30 minutes. Skim off the resulting foam several times. In the end, sift the ingredients through a cloth.

Refrigerate for later use

9.9 Basic recipe for a reissue soup (Congee)

Low fat content, for the drainage of the body overweight and high blood pressure.
Cooking time approx. 2-4 hours
3 portions to 273,33g. / 140kcal. - (carb:90% / prot:10%)
100g.=51,34kcal. / protein 2,96g. fat:0,48g.
µg. - Ph:1,95 Na:0,19 Ka:1,67 Mg:1,14 Ca:0,57 Fe:0,01 Zn:0,02 Col.:0 Hsr.:2,11

Quantity of ingredients:
Rice variety any 1 cup / 120g. (yes)
Water 6 cups / 700g. (yes)

Cooking instructions:
Cook rice and water in a ratio of about 1: 6. The amount of water determines the thickness of the mash (matter of taste).
Put the rice in a saucepan with a heavy lid. It is important to simmer the rice after a short boil on the slightest flame, otherwise it burns.
Boil the rice for 2-4 hours. The longer he cooks, the more he strengthens.
If you want to eat the dish for breakfast, you can put the rice on just before bedtime.
To be on the safe side, you should first check the behavior of your pot and cooker under observation for a similar amount of time, so that nothing burns.
Refrigerate for later use.

9.10 Basic recipe for a vegetable soup, nutritious

Reduces blood pressure, strengthens immune system, prevents cancer, forcing spleen, dissolves stagnation, promotes weight loss. Good to fight immunodeficiency, high blood pressure, depressions, diabetes, diarrhea, reduces blood lipids.
Cooking time approx. 2-3 hours
Allergens: L
5 portions to 240,6g. / 48kcal. - (carb:71% / prot:29%)
100g.=19,87kcal. / protein 1,56g. fat:1,31g.
µg. - Ph:0,97 Na:0,73 Ka:5,14 Mg:0,36 Ca:1,26 Fe:0,02 Zn:0,01 Col.:0 Hsr.:0,56

Quantity of ingredients:
Olive oil 1 table spoon / 4g. (yes)
Onion white 1 piece / 60g. (yes)
Carrot 3 pieces / 200g. (yes)
Parsnip 3/8 lbs - 6oz / 150g. (yes)
Celery root 1 cup / 100g. (yes)

Ginger fresh 1/2 teaspoon / 2g. (yes)
Lemon 1/2 piece / 25g. (yes)
Juniper berry 6 pieces / 6g. (yes)
Thyme dried 1 pinch / 1g. (yes)
Lovage 1 table spoon / 3g. (yes)
Bay leaf 2 leaves / 1g. (yes)
Salt 1 pinch / 1g. (little)
Water 3 cups / 650g. (yes)

Cooking instructions:
Cut the vegetables into cubes.
Heat oil in hot pot, fry shortly onions and vegetables.
Add cold water, then add ginger, bay leaf and lemon juice.
Season with juniper, thyme and lovage. Cover for 2 - 3 hours on a low heat and simmer.
The used vegetables should be thrown away.
The basic recipe serves as a soup base and to refine vegetables, legumes or cereals.
If you want to eat vegetable soup immediately, add the desired vegetables half an hour before.
Refrigerate for later use.

9.11 Black root with yogurt

Stimulates kidney, bladder and forces the cleaning of the body. In the physiological sense, they generally stimulate the glands in the organism. Good to fight acute or chronic constipation of the intestine. Rich in Vitamins and trace elements.
Cooking time approx. 20 min
Allergens: AG
2 portions to 303g. / 266kcal. - (carb:77% / prot:23%)
100g.=87,95kcal. / protein 7,92g. fat:2,06g.
µg. - Ph:45,47 Na:46,64 Ka:135,46 Mg:13,05 Ca:29,93 Fe:1,29 Zn:0,23 Col.:0,33
Hsr.:28,98

Quantity of ingredients:
Salsify 1 lbs / 400g. (yes)
Yogurt (natural, 1.5% fat) 4 table spoons / 80g. (yes)
Salt 1 pinch / 1g. (little)
Multi-grain bread (gray bread) 6 slices / 120g. (yes)
Herbs various 1 handful / 5g. (yes)

Cooking instructions:
Peel the salsify and simmer in salted water until tender. Pour away the water, cool the salsify and cut it to size. Cover with yoghurt and sprinkle with fresh herbs. Serve with the bread.
You can also use the salsify from the conserve.

9.12 Breakfast - Rice with fruits

Good to fight blood circulation disorders, thrombose, risk of embolism, high blood pressure, a headache, heart attack and stroke. Encourages blood build-up, promotes digestion, reduces Inflammation.
Cooking time approx. 10 min - 3 hours
Allergens: GHO
3 portions to 282g. / 231kcal. - (carb:90% / prot:10%)
100g.=81,8kcal. / protein 3,59g. fat:7,61g.
µg. - Ph:3,19 Na:0,7 Ka:8,57 Mg:20,72 Ca:21,22 Fe:0,05 Zn:0,02 Col.:0,54 Hsr.:0,92

Quantity of ingredients:
Basic recipe for a rice soup (Congee) 6 cups / 500g. (yes)
Cow's milk (whole milk 3.5% fat) 1/2 to 1 cup / 80g. (yes)
Honey 1 table spoon / 10g. (little)
Butter organic 1 table spoon / 15g. (little)
Dates dried 1 table spoon / 15g. (little)
Fig 1 table spoon / 15g. (yes)
Apple (sour) 1 piece / 200g. (yes)
Hazelnuts 1/2 teaspoon / 5g. (yes)
Almond 1/2 teaspoon / 5g. (yes)
Cinnamon ground 1 pinch / 1g. (yes)

Cooking instructions:
Cook rice congee according to basic recipe or use pre-cooked.
Make it with the milk more fluid, and sweet with honey.
Fry the fruits and nuts in butter and mix with the finished rice soup, add chopped dates, figs and the apple.

9.13 Broccoli and Parmesan spread on toast bread

Good to fight loss of appetite, blood clotting, thyroid function, increase Vitamin B12, strengthen immune system, good to fight belching, diabetes, acute or chronic constipation, dissolves stagnation.
Cooking time approx. 15 min
Allergens: AG
2 portions to 170,5g. / 148kcal. - (carb:29% / prot:71%)
100g.=86,8kcal. / protein 12,1g. fat:11,33g.
µg. - Ph:34,79 Na:27,37 Ka:60,2 Mg:5,76 Ca:40,04 Fe:0,24 Zn:0,19 Col.:1,88 Hsr.:6,09

Quantity of ingredients:
Broccoli 5/8 oz / 200g. (yes)
Curd cheese 20% 3 oz / 80g. (yes)
Yogurt (natural, 1.5% fat) 1 table spoon / 10g. (yes)
Parmesan 2 table spoons / 15g. (little)
Lemon peel 1/2 teaspoon / 1g. (yes)
Basil (fresh) 1 table spoon / 5g. (yes)
Chives 1 table spoon / 5g. (yes)
Salt 1 pinch / 1g. (little)
Pepper (ground) 1 pinch / 0,3g. ()
Toast bread (whole grain) 6 slices / 24g. (yes)

Cooking instructions:
Cook broccoli in a sieve insert over steam for 8 minutes until firm. Finely chop broccoli.
Mix the curd, yoghurt, parmesan and lemon peel well. Mix cheese cream with broccoli, basil and chives. Season the spread with salt and pepper. Serve on the crunchy toasted toast.

9.14 Broccoli cream soup

Strengthen your immune system, build and maintain healthy bones, teeth, hair and nails. Reduces blood pressure, strengthens immune system, prevents cancer, reduces radiation damage.
Cooking time approx. 30 min
Allergens: LO
6 portions to 251,17g. / 98kcal. - (carb:79% / prot:21%)
100g.=39,02kcal. / protein 4,17g. fat:1,91g.
µg. - Ph:1,14 Na:0,45 Ka:4,37 Mg:1,39 Ca:5,42 Fe:0,03 Zn:0,01 Col.:0 Hsr.:0,45

Quantity of ingredients:
Olive oil 2 table spoons / 7g. (yes)
Broccoli 1,1 lbs / 500g. (yes)
Carrot 2 pieces / 150g. (yes)
Potato 2 pieces / 120g. (yes)
Onion white 1 piece / 50g. (yes)
Water 1 cup / 50g. (yes)
Basic recipe for a vegetable soup (nutritious) 2 cup / 500g. (yes)
White wine 1/2 cup / 125g. (little)
Sage 1 teaspoon / 2g. (yes)
Rosemary 1 teaspoon / 2g. (yes)
Pepper (ground) 1 pinch / 0,5g. ()
Salt 1 pinch / 1g. (little)

Cooking instructions:
Add the olive oil to the pan, add the washed and cut broccoli, diced carrots and potatoes, sauté for a short time, add the chopped onion, fill with water, enough water to cover the vegetables at least 3 finger breadths. Add bouillon, salt, add a little bit of white wine, add the seasoned sage and rosemary.
Heat till it boils and then simmer on a small fire for about 25 minutes.
Season with pepper, if necessary season with sea salt. Purée the soup.

9.15 Carp soup

Increase milk production and sweating, dissolves stagnation, reduces blood pressure, strengthens immune system, improves blood circulation, improves medication effect, stimulates appetite. Strengthens gastrointestinal function, expands blood vessels.
Cooking time approx. 2 hours
Allergens: DO
6 portions to 316,5g. / 166kcal. - (carb:28% / prot:72%)
100g.=52,55kcal. / protein 17,89g. fat:4,48g.
µg. - Ph:2,23 Na:1,04 Ka:3,86 Mg:0,52 Ca:1,11 Fe:0,01 Zn:0,01 Col.:0,61 Hsr.:14,01

Quantity of ingredients:
Carp 1,1 lbs / 500g. (yes)
Salt 1 pinch / 1g. (little)
Vinegar (Apple vinegar) 1 teaspoon / 3g. (yes)
Thyme 1 Twig / 3g. (yes)
Juniper berry 8 pieces / 3g. (yes)
Carrot 2 pieces / 200g. (yes)
Leek 1 piece / 200g. (yes)
Onion white 1 piece / 60g. (yes)
Ginger fresh 1/2 teaspoon / 2g. (yes)
Bay leaf 3 leaves / 1g. (yes)
White wine 1/2 cup / 125g. (little)
Basil 3 leaves / 1g. (yes)
Water 4 cup / 800g. (yes)

Cooking instructions:
Preparation: When shopping at the fishmonger, remove the fillets from a medium-sized, whole carp and also pack the fish head, spine with bones and tail.

Cut the fillets into 1 cm cubes; salt and set aside.

Place fish head, backbone and tail of carp in plenty of cold water; heat till it boils and scoop the foam; add a dash of vinegar, a fresh sprig of thyme, juniper berries; Add carrot, a piece of leek and chopped onion; add a thick slice of ginger, some peppercorns, 1 bay leaf, salt; simmer for about 1 1/2 hours and pour the stock through a sieve.

Put the carp pieces in a saucepan; pour a shot of white wine; Add rose paprika, basil leaves, finely ground carrots, dried thyme and the stock and warm; Boil the ingredients for about 5 minutes until the fish pieces are cooked.
Variants: Thicken the soup with kudzu or mashed potatoes.
This fits: baguette and dry white wine.

9.16 Carrot drink

Promotes spleen and liver, reduces blood pressure, strengthens immune system, prevents cancer, reduces radiation damage, diuretic, building up, eye-enhancing, detoxifying, nerve-strengthening.
Cooking time approx. 15 min
Allergens: H
1 portion to 265g. / 143kcal. - (carb:81% / prot:19%)
100g.=53,96kcal. / protein 3,78g. fat:2,5g.
µg. - Ph:43,4 Na:22,3 Ka:117,79 Mg:18,2 Ca:36,26 Fe:1,83 Zn:0,55 Col.:0 Hsr.:17,98

Quantity of ingredients:
Millet flakes 1 table spoon / 10g. (yes)
Carrot 7/8 lbs / 200g. (yes)
Almond puree 1 teaspoon / 3g. (yes)
Honey 1/2 teaspoon / 2g. (little)
Water 1/4 cup / 50g. (yes)

Cooking instructions:
Sprinkle millet flakes with 50 ml of cold water and let it swell for 10 minutes.
Juice the fresh carrots or use 200 ml. carrot juice.
Puree the millet flakes, carrot juice, almond paste and honey with the blender.

9.17 Carrot Risotto

Strengthens immune system, prevents cancer, loss of appetite, flatulence, high blood pressure, depressions, diabetes, diarrhea, stimulates liver function, dissolves stagnation.
Cooking time approx. 45 min
Allergens: GL
2 portions to 340,5g. / 308kcal. - (carb:84% / prot:16%)
100g.=90,46kcal. / protein 8,49g. fat:5,98g.
µg. - Ph:13,57 Na:9,57 Ka:29,14 Mg:16,17 Ca:58,13 Fe:0,33 Zn:0,11 Col.:0,3 Hsr.:7,34

Quantity of ingredients:
Olive oil 1/2 teaspoon / 5g. (yes)
Onion (spring onion) 2 table spoons / 7g. (yes)
Nutmeg 1 pinch / 0,3g. (yes)
Parsley 1/2 bunch / 25g. (yes)
Rice variety any 1/4 lbs - 4oz / 100g. (yes)
Carrot 5/8 lbs - 8oz / 250g. (yes)
Basic recipe for a vegetable soup (nutritious) 1 cup / 280g. (yes)
Fennel seeds ground 1/4 teaspoon / 1g. (yes)
Basil (fresh) 1/2 teaspoon / 2g. (yes)
Salt 1 pinch / 1g. (little)
Pepper (ground) 1 pinch / 0,3g. ()
Parmesan 1 table spoon / 10g. (little)

Cooking instructions:
Heat the oil in a pan, fry the onions in a glassy and very soft manner. Add parsley, sauté briefly. Add rice, carrots and nutmeg, sauté briefly while stirring. Add the vegetable stock, season with fennel and basil, heat till it boils and cook for about 20 minutes until the rice and carrots are well. Stir from time to time and add some vegetable stock if necessary. The risotto should be slightly soupy. Just before the end of the cooking time mix in the white wine and simmer the risotto for a short while. Remove risotto from the heat, mix in Parmesan.

9.18 Carrot soup

Promotes spleen and liver, reduces blood pressure, strengthens immune system, prevents cancer, reduces radiation damage, improves blood circulation, improves medication effect, increase Appetite, stimulates liver function.
Cooking time approx. 30 min
Allergens: O

4 portions to 275,75g. / 105kcal. - (carb:71% / prot:29%)
100g.=37,99kcal. / protein 2,47g. fat:2,63g.
µg. - Ph:1,6 Na:1,04 Ka:5,89 Mg:0,68 Ca:1,62 Fe:0,07 Zn:0,02 Col.:0 Hsr.:2,36

Quantity of ingredients:
Carrot 1,1 lbs / 500g. (yes)
Pepper (ground) 1 pinch / 0,5g. ()
Nutmeg 1 pinch / 1g. (yes)
Salt 1 pinch / 1g. (little)
White wine 1/2 cup / 125g. (little)
Orange juice Alternatively for wine / 0g. (little)
Parsley 2 table spoons / 10g. (yes)
Peppers powder 1 pinch / 1g. (yes)
Thyme dried Alternative to rose paprika / 0g. (yes)
Pine nuts 1 table spoon / 15g. (yes)
Sunflower seeds Alternatively to pine nuts / 0g. (yes)
Water 2 cup / 450g. (yes)

Cooking instructions:
Place peeled large cut carrot pieces in hot water; cook and then puree;
season with ground pepper, a little nutmeg,
a pinch of salt; add a dash of white wine and simmer for a few minutes
or season with orange juice; Add parsley as desired; stir in some rose
paprika or fresh thyme; sprinkle with roasted pine nuts or sunflower
seeds before serving.

9.19 Celery and potato cream soup

Reduces blood pressure, strengthens immune system, promotes weight
loss. Good to fight immunodeficiency, loss of appetite, flatulence,
depressions, diabetes, diarrhea, improves digestion.
Cooking time approx. 45 min
Allergens: GL
4 portions to 241,5g. / 113kcal. - (carb:83% / prot:17%)
100g.=46,69kcal. / protein 2,15g. fat:5,52g.
µg. - Ph:5,96 Na:3,46 Ka:23,98 Mg:22,27 Ca:83,51 Fe:0,18 Zn:0,01 Col.:0 Hsr.:1,49

Quantity of ingredients:
Olive oil 1 table spoon / 10g. (yes)
Onion white 1/2 piece / 25g. (yes)
Basic recipe for a vegetable soup (nutritious) 3 cups / 700g. (yes)
Potato 5/8 oz / 200g. (yes)
Nutmeg 1 pinch / 0,5g. (yes)
Ground 1 pinch / 0,5g. (yes)

Lemon peel 1/4 piece / 1g. (yes)
Crème fraiche cheese 2 table spoons / 20g. (little)
Salt 1 pinch / 1g. (little)
Parsley 1 table spoon / 8g. (yes)

Cooking instructions:
Heat the olive oil in a saucepan lightly. Fry the onions very gently in a mild heat. Pour with vegetable stock according to the basic recipe. Cover and cook for 15 minutes.
Add curd-cut potato, celery, nutmeg, cumin and lemon zest. Spice with salt and cook for 12 minutes. Potatoes and celery should be soft. Remove the lemon peel.
Puree the soup with crème fraiche using a blender. Season the soup with salt. Arrange the soup in portions with the chopped parsley.

9.20 Champignon salad with cress

Promotes digestion and is good to fight high blood pressure. Good to fight loss of appetite, improves blood circulation.
Cooking time approx. 5 min
Allergens: AN
1 portion to 312g. / 220kcal. - (carb:56% / prot:44%)
100g.=70,51kcal. / protein 9,74g. fat:7,08g.
µg. - Ph:105,24 Na:37,35 Ka:366,67 Mg:14,25 Ca:19,03 Fe:1,08 Zn:0,41 Col.:0,02 Hsr.:60,22

Quantity of ingredients:
Champignon 5/8 lbs - 8oz / 250g. (yes)
Sesame oil 2 table spoons / 6g. (yes)
Pepper (ground) 1 pinch / 0,5g. ()
Salt 1 pinch / 1g. (little)
Lemon 1/2 piece / 15g. (yes)
Peppers powder 2 pinches / 0,1g. (yes)
Cress 2 table spoons / 10g. (yes)
White bread (wheat bread) 2 slices / 30g. (little)

Cooking instructions:
Cut mushrooms into thin slices.
Dressing: sesame oil, a little ground pepper, salt, plenty of lemon juice, stir well the rose pepper; give over the finely chopped mushrooms; plenty of watercress.
Goes well with: white bread, round grain rice or quinoa; Along with the cereal, the salad makes a simple, light meal.
Serve with white bread.

9.21 Chicken soup with egg yolk and parsley

Strengthens blood, strengthens bone marrow, reduces blood pressure, strengthens immune system. Parsley stimulates liver function, harmonizes liver and spleen, strengthens eyesight, detoxifying.
Cooking time approx. 10 min
Allergens: CL
2 portions to 260g. / 118kcal. - (carb:82% / prot:18%)
100g.=45,19kcal. / protein 16,35g. fat:2,49g.
µg. - Ph:6,98 Na:8,83 Ka:9 Mg:24,79 Ca:69,4 Fe:0,28 Zn:0,05 Col.:6,52 Hsr.:2,22

Quantity of ingredients:
Basic recipe for a chicken soup (warming) 2 cup / 500g. (yes)
Chicken yolk 1 piece / 10g. (yes)
Parsley 1 table spoon / 10g. (yes)

Cooking instructions:
Cook the chicken broth according to the basic recipe.
Heat broth and bubble the egg yolk. Sprinkle the chopped parsley over it and let it rest for about 2 minutes. Drink in small sips.

9.22 Cocoa with cardamom

Builds up liver, strengthens muscles, lowers blood pressure. Antioxidant, rich in vital substances. Slightly laxative. Promotes digestion.
Cooking time approx. 5 min.
Allergens: G
2 portions to 533g. / 350kcal. - (carb:66% / prot:34%)
100g.=65,67kcal. / protein 17,84g. fat:8,81g.
µg. - Ph:60,04 Na:23,87 Ka:116,01 Mg:15,45 Ca:59,34 Fe:0,35 Zn:0,16 Col.:1,41
Hsr.:0,49

Quantity of ingredients:
Cocoa 50 g. / 50g. (rec.)
Vanilla pod 1 piece / 0,5g. (yes)
Cow's milk (1.5% fat) 4 cup / 1000g. (yes)
Sugar white 4 table spoons / 15g. (little)
Cardamom 1 pinch / 1g. (yes)

Cooking instructions:
Mix the cocoa powder with the sugar, the pith of the vanilla pod, cardamom and 4-5 tablespoons of cold milk. Heat the milk in a pan (do not boil), stir in the cocoa with the whisk.

9.23 Colorful rice dish

Strengthens immune system, good to fight diabetes, strengthens spleen and stomach, strengthens blood, strengthens the muscles, tendons and bones, promotes digestion, helps to digest fat, supports urination, reduces blood pressure, dissolves stagnation.
Cooking time approx. 45 min
Allergens: L
3 portions to 342,67g. / 437kcal. - (carb:63% / prot:37%)
100g.=127,63kcal. / protein 17,03g. fat:10,23g.
µg. - Ph:7,97 Na:4,89 Ka:17,25 Mg:6,38 Ca:18,08 Fe:0,14 Zn:0,11
Col.:1 Hsr.:5,14

Quantity of ingredients:
Olive oil 2 teaspoons / 20g. (yes)
Onion (spring onion) 1 piece / 20g. (yes)
Beef meat 1/4 lbs - 4oz / 125g. (yes)
Rice (whole grain) 3 oz / 80g. (yes)
Basic recipe for a vegetable soup (nutritious) 1 cup / 300g. (yes)
Celery root 1/8 lbs - 2oz / 50g. (yes)
Leek 1 piece / 100g. (yes)
Beans (green; fresh) 3/8 lbs - 6oz / 150g. (yes)
Carrot 1 piece / 70g. (yes)
Tomato 2 pieces / 100g. (yes)
Salt 1 pinch / 0,5g. (little)
Pepper (ground) 1 pinch / 0,2g. ()
Herbs various 2 table spoons / 12g. (yes)

Cooking instructions:
Wash leek and carrots, clean and chop them. Dice the celery, slice the tomatoes.

Fry in a large, deep pan with oil, onion and minced meat.

Add brown rice and prepared vegetables (celery, leeks, beans, carrots, tomatoes). Braise briefly.

Season with salt, pepper and paprika. Add vegetable broth. Heat till it boils and cook over low heat for 20 to 30 minutes with the lid closed.

Sprinkle with fresh chopped herbs and serve.

9.24 Compote of pears

Pear benefits digestion, supports urination. Cocoa forces liver, strengthens the muscles, strengthens the defense. Good to fight fungi infections.
Cooking time approx. 10 min
4 portions to 270,75g. / 122kcal. - (carb:93% / prot:7%)
100g.=45,24kcal. / protein 1,27g. fat:0,86g.
µg. - Ph:0,76 Na:0,11 Ka:6,01 Mg:0,38 Ca:0,62 Fe:0,01 Zn:0,01 Col.:0 Hsr.:0,69

Quantity of ingredients:
Water 1 cup / 280g. (yes)
Pear 4 pieces / 800g. (yes)
Anise (Common Fennel) 1/2 teaspoon / 1g. (yes)
Vanilla pod 1 pinch / 1g. (yes)
Chili (pod or ground) very little / 0,2g. (yes)
Cocoa 1 pinch / 1g. (rec.)

Cooking instructions:
Boil pears (organic - with peel), aniseed, vanilla, chili soft. Sprinkle with cocoa.

9.25 Couscous Salad

Prevents cancer, forcing spleen, promotes digestion, stimulates liver function, reduces blood pressure, strengthens immune system, reduces radiation damage, diuretic.
Cooking time approx. 25 min
Allergens: A
3 portions to 285,67g. / 338kcal. - (carb:75% / prot:25%)
100g.=118,32kcal. / protein 12,21g. fat:7,11g.
µg. - Ph:5,1 Na:5,76 Ka:27,89 Mg:2,17 Ca:7,1 Fe:0,15 Zn:0,07 Col.:0 Hsr.:4,56

Quantity of ingredients:
Water 1 cup / 100g. (yes)
Olive oil 1 table spoon / 15g. (yes)
Couscous 5/8 oz / 200g. (yes)
Lemon juice 3 table spoons / 30g. (yes)
Lemon peel 1 teaspoon / 2g. (yes)
Tomato 2 pieces / 80g. (yes)
Cucumber 1/4 lbs - 4oz / 100g. (yes)
Carrot 1/4 lbs - 4oz / 100g. (yes)
Parsley 1 Bunch / 100g. (yes)
Chives 1 Bunch / 100g. (yes)
Peppermint 3 twigs / 30g. (yes)

Cooking instructions:
Boil in a small saucepan 250 ml. water with salt and 1 tablespoon olive oil. Add the couscous, take the stove in the front and let it swell covered for 5 minutes. Put the couscous back on the stove and let it simmer for about 2 minutes with gentle stirring. If necessary, add 1 - 3 tbsp of hot water.
Mix the couscous with lemon juice, chopped lemon peel and 1 tbsp oil, season with salt and pepper and leave to set.
Add couscous with tomatoes, cucumber, parsley (all diced), carrots (grated), chives and mint (finely chopped). Season the couscous salad with lemon juice, salt and pepper.

9.26 Cranberry yogurt mix

Good to fight acute or chronic constipation of the intestine, oral mucosal inflammation, diarrhea, flatulence, throat irritation.
Cooking time approx. 5 min
Allergens: GO
2 portions to 197,5g. / 57kcal. - (carb:75% / prot:25%)
100g.=28,86kcal. / protein 2,13g. fat:1,02g.
µg. - Ph:7,17 Na:5,87 Ka:13,16 Mg:2,71 Ca:16,61 Fe:0,01 Zn:0,03 Col.:0,39 Hsr.:0,2

Quantity of ingredients:
Yogurt (natural, 1.5% fat) 1/4 lbs - 4oz / 125g. (yes)
Cranberry jam 2 table spoons / 20g. (little)
Mineral water 1 cup / 250g. (yes)

Cooking instructions:
Mix yoghurt, cranberry jam and mineral water until frothy.

9.27 Cream cheese substitute

Good to fight lactose intolerance. Strengthens body energy, promotes digestion, promotes weight loss. Good to fight immunodeficiency, loss of appetite, arteriosclerosis, flatulence, bladder weakness, anemia, high blood pressure, depressions, diabetes, diarrhea.
Cooking time approx. 20 min
Allergens: AE
2 portions to 328g. / 526kcal. - (carb:64% / prot:36%)
100g.=160,37kcal. / protein 19,62g. fat:12,75g.
µg. - Ph:32,54 Na:139,79 Ka:55,62 Mg:9,78 Ca:5,31 Fe:0,41 Zn:0,33 Col.:0 Hsr.:16,16

Quantity of ingredients:
Soybean milk 4 cup / 300g. (yes)
Lemon 1 piece / 50g. (yes)
Herbs various 2 table spoons / 6g. (yes)
Whole grain bread 6 slices / 300g. (yes)

Cooking instructions:
Heat the soy milk in a saucepan till it boils, stirring occasionally (gets burn easily!), Then allow to cool.
Squeeze out the lemon and stir gently under the cooled soy milk (approx. 80°C/176°F), let it approx. 20 min. rest or clot.
Pour chopped soy milk through a strainer lined with a dishcloth, allow liquid to drain and then squeeze out remaining liquid with the dishcloth.
Refine to taste with fresh herbs.
(Serve with wholemeal bread.)

9.28 Cucumber salad

Diuretic, detoxifying, suppresses conversion of sugar into fat, lowers cholesterol, prevents cancer. Cucumber cools and moistens. Dill works against flatulence, anticonvulsant in gastrointestinal discomfort.
Cooking time approx. 5 min
Allergens: O
2 portions to 206g. / 27kcal. - (carb:68% / prot:32%)
100g.=13,11kcal. / protein 1,61g. fat:0,4g.
µg. - Ph:5,92 Na:2,32 Ka:35,15 Mg:2,16 Ca:4,03 Fe:0,12 Zn:0,05 Col.:0 Hsr.:1,94

Quantity of ingredients:
Cucumber 1 piece / 400g. (yes)
Salt 1 pinch / 1g. (little)
Dill 1 pinch / 1g. (yes)
Vinegar (Apple vinegar) 1 table spoon / 10g. (yes)

Cooking instructions:
Cut the cucumber (do not peel the BIO) thinly and season.

9.29 Fennel and potato gratin

Reduces inflammation, improves blood circulation, improves digestion, supports urination, lowers cholesterol, good to fight loss of appetite, flatulence, inflammatory bowel disease, heartburn. Forcing spleen, improves blood circulation.

Cooking time approx. 1 1/2 hours
Allergens: CGL
2 portions to 230,5g. / 147kcal. - (carb:68% / prot:32%)
100g.=63,77kcal. / protein 5,72g. fat:5,42g.
μg. - Ph:15 Na:12,98 Ka:80,91 Mg:13,52 Ca:40,41 Fe:0,41 Zn:0,09 Col.:7,81 Hsr.:3,64

Quantity of ingredients:
Fennel 5/8 oz / 200g. (yes)
Potato 1/4 lbs - 4oz / 125g. (yes)
Basic recipe for a vegetable soup (nutritious) 1/2 cup / 100g. (yes)
Butter organic 1 teaspoon / 3g. (little)
Rice flour 2 teaspoons / 6g. (yes)
Cream sour 10% 1 teaspoon / 3g. (yes)
Salt 1 pinch / 1g. (little)
Sugar cane sugar 1 pinch / 1g. (little)
Chicken yolk 1 piece / 10g. (yes)
Pepper Cayenne 1 pinch / 0,5g. (yes)
Nutmeg 1 pinch / 0,5g. (yes)
Parsley 1 teaspoon / 2g. (yes)
Chives 1 teaspoon / 3g. (yes)
Parmesan 1 teaspoon / 3g. (little)
Butter organic 1 teaspoon / 3g. (little)

Cooking instructions:
Cook peeled potatoes and then let cool. Wash the fennel, cut off the stems and remove any outer leaves.
Hold back fennel greens and add it to the sauce with the other herbs later.
Steam the fennel tubers for about 15 - 20 minutes.
Then cut the potatoes and fennel into slices and place in layers in a greased baking dish.
Bring the liquid of fennel broth to the boil and bind it with flour.
Season with sea salt, cayenne pepper, sugar, nutmeg and sour cream. Allow to cool and alloy with egg yolk.
Spread the sauce over the casserole, sprinkle with parmesan and finely chopped parsley and chives. Bake at 200 °C / 392 °F in the oven for half an hour.

9.30 Fine Russian borscht

Strengths spleen and stomach, strengthens the heart, stimulates digestion, reduces blood pressure, strengthens immune system. For strengthening after diseases. Good to fight bloating, cramping in gastrointestinal complaints.

Cooking time approx. 30 min

Allergens: AGLO

6 portions to 368,33g. / 172kcal. - (carb:81% / prot:19%)
100g.=46,61kcal. / protein 6,07g. fat:3,32g.
µg. - Ph:1,04 Na:1,82 Ka:4,72 Mg:1,22 Ca:4,74 Fe:0,02 Zn:0 Col.:0,01 Hsr.:0,78

Quantity of ingredients:
Red beet 5/8 oz / 200g. (yes)
Sunflower oil 1 table spoon / 10g. (yes)
Onion (shallot) 2 pieces / 40g. (yes)
Carrot 2 pieces / 140g. (yes)
Celery root 1 piece / 500g. (yes)
Parsley root 1 piece / 150g. (yes)
Leek 1/8 lbs - 2oz / 50g. (yes)
Basic recipe for a vegetable soup (nutritious) 3 cups / 650g. (yes)
Bay leaf 1 Leaf / 0,2g. (yes)
Juniper berry 2 pieces / 2g. (yes)
Nutmeg 1 pinch / 1g. (yes)
Savoy cabbage / kale 5/8 oz / 200g. (yes)
Salt 1 pinch / 1g. (little)
Pepper (ground) 1 pinch / 0,5g. ()
Ground 1 pinch / 1g. (yes)
Red wine 1/2 cup / 125g. (little)
Sour cream 15% fat 1 table spoon / 10g. (little)
Dill 1 teaspoon / 10g. (yes)
White bread (wheat bread) 6 slices / 120g. (little)

Cooking instructions:
Fry some beetroot in oil. Fry the onions, carrots, celery, parsley root and leek well in another pan. Add the stock and the wine; then add bay leaves, juniper berries and nutmeg and simmer for 15 minutes. Remove the bay leaf and puree everything.
Heat more broth separately, simmer the steamed beetroot in it. Add cabbage or white cabbage after half the cooking time and let it steep. At the end, add the pureed vegetables and season with salt, pepper, ground cumin and a little red wine. Garnish with some sour cream and finely chopped dill in the plate. Serve with a slice of white bread.

9.31 Fish soup with rosemary

Promotes spleen and liver, reduces blood pressure, strengthens immune system, prevents cancer, reduces radiation damage, has little cholesterol and is protein rich, improves blood circulation, increases appetite. Antioxidant, forcing spleen, dissolves stagnation.
Cooking time approx. 30 min
Allergens: DLO
4 portions to 284,25g. / 271kcal. - (carb:38% / prot:62%)
100g.=95,43kcal. / protein 15,39g. fat:14,78g.
µg. - Ph:4,93 Na:1,8 Ka:11,89 Mg:0,76 Ca:1,33 Fe:0,03 Zn:0,03 Col.:0,01 Hsr.:3,59

Quantity of ingredients:
Basic recipe for a fish soup 2 cup / 500g. (yes)
Rosemary 1/2 bunch / 7g. (yes)
Onion (spring onion) 1 piece / 20g. (yes)
Olive oil 2 table spoons / 35g. (yes)
Fish pieces mixed (fresh water) 5/8 lbs - 8oz / 250g. (yes)
Carrot 1 piece / 120g. (yes)
Parsnip 1 piece / 180g. (yes)
Celery root 1 slice / 20g. (yes)
Salt 1 pinch / 1g. (little)
Peppercorns 2 pieces / 1g. (yes)
Garlic 1 clove / 3g. (yes)

Cooking instructions:
Fry the onion and garlic in oil. Add fish broth. Add diced carrots, parsnips and celery. Season with salt and peppercorns. Simmer the soup on a low heat for 25 minutes.
Wash the fish, drizzle with lemon juice, divide into pieces and add to the soup with the pink rosemary. Cook for 5 min on low heat.
Add the chives and parsley and season the soup with the salt.

9.32 Fruit juice

Stops diarrhea, promotes digestion, appetizing, harmonizes the stomach, relieves pain, detoxifying, reduces blood pressure, strengthens immune system, prevents cancer, reduces radiation damage.
Cooking time approx. 10 min
2 portions to 305g. / 176kcal. - (carb:93% / prot:7%)
100g.=57,54kcal. / protein 1,89g. fat:0,9g.
µg. - Ph:4,99 Na:2,24 Ka:37,45 Mg:2,36 Ca:6,04 Fe:0,21 Zn:0,05 Col.:0 Hsr.:4,3

Quantity of ingredients:
Orange 2 pieces / 150g. (yes)
Apple (sweet) 4 pieces / 300g. (yes)
Carrot 2 pieces / 150g. (yes)
Honey 1 table spoon / 10g. (little)

Cooking instructions:
Peel oranges and carrots. Cut all ingredients into cubes so that they fit into the juicer and juice. Sweet with honey.

9.33 Halibut with tomato and garlic sauce

Promotes digestion, helps to digest fat, supports urination, reduces blood pressure, good to fight rheumatism, flatulence, bladder weakness, anemia, high blood pressure, depressions, diabetes, diarrhea. Valuable omega-3 fatty acids.
Cooking time approx. 45 min
Allergens: D
5 portions to 297,6g. / 319kcal. - (carb:36% / prot:64%)
100g.=107,19kcal. / protein 34,96g. fat:9,44g.
µg. - Ph:4,82 Na:8,78 Ka:7,08 Mg:1,03 Ca:0,88 Fe:0,02 Zn:0,01 Col.:0,82 Hsr.:4,78

Quantity of ingredients:
Rice variety any 1 cup / 120g. (yes)
Water 6 cups / 240g. (yes)
Salt 1 pinch / 1g. (little)
Halibut (Flatfish) 2,2 lbs / 800g. (yes)
Salt 1 pinch / 1g. (little)
Pepper (ground) 1 pinch / 0,5g. ()
Lemon juice 1 splash / 2g. (yes)
Bay leaf 2 pieces / 2g. (yes)
Lemon 1 piece / 30g. (yes)
Garlic 8 pieces / 10g. (yes)
Thyme dried 1 table spoon / 5g. (yes)
Olives 0,2 lbs / 75g. (yes)
Tomato 4 pieces / 200g. (yes)
Salt 1 pinch / 1g. (little)
Pepper (ground) 1 pinch / 0,5g. ()

Cooking instructions:
Cook rice with salted water (1:3).
Rinse the fish under running cold water, dab with kitchen paper and rub with salt, pepper and lemon juice.
Place the fish fillets in a casserole dish with pieces of bay leaf.

Wash the lemon hot and cut into slices, peel and halve the garlic.
Sprinkle the olives and the thyme over them.
Brew the tomatoes with hot water, skin and chop.
Mix all ingredients, season with salt and pepper and distribute around the fish. Cook everything at 200°C/392°F for about 20 minutes.
Serve with the rice.

9.34 Kohlrabi in chervil sauce with potatoes

Reduces inflammation, lowers cholesterol, diuretic, conducts bowel winds, strengthens immune system, prevents cancer, promotes weight loss. Good to fight loss of appetite, flatulence, high blood pressure, depressions, diabetes, diarrhea.
Cooking time approx. 1 hour
Allergens: GL
4 portions to 316,75g. / 188kcal. - (carb:79% / prot:21%)
100g.=59,19kcal. / protein 8,66g. fat:2,51g.
µg. - Ph:2,95 Na:1,03 Ka:25,06 Mg:3,48 Ca:15,16 Fe:0,04 Zn:0,02 Col.:0,06 Hsr.:0,91

Quantity of ingredients:
Potato 6 pieces / 450g. (yes)
Basic recipe for a vegetable soup (nutritious) 1 cup / 300g. (yes)
Potato 1/4 lbs - 4oz / 100g. (yes)
Nutmeg 1 pinch / 0,2g. (yes)
Lemon peel 1/2 teaspoon / 2g. (yes)
Ginger fresh 1/2 teaspoon / 2g. (yes)
Lovage 1/2 teaspoon / 2g. (yes)
Kohlrabi 3/4 lbs / 300g. (yes)
Salt 1 pinch / 1g. (little)
Pepper (ground) 1 pinch / 0,2g. ()
Sour cream 15% fat 3 table spoons / 30g. (little)
Chervil dried 1 Bunch / 80g. (yes)

Cooking instructions:
Boil the potatoes in salted water.
Bring half of the vegetable stock to boil. Add the diced potatoes, nutmeg, lemon zest, ginger and lovage. Cover the potatoes and cook for about 10 minutes until soft and puree them with a blender until they are smooth.
Bring remaining vegetable stock to boil. Cut kohlrabi into cubes and add, cover and cook for about 8 minutes. Stir in the potato sauce and heat everything briefly. Puree with the mixing stick chervil and sour cream. Mix the chervil cream with the kohlrabi vegetables. Serve with the cooked, peeled potatoes.

9.35 Lettuce with fresh cheese

The bitter substances have diuretic effect and promote the blood circulation in the digestive area. Mustard improves thyroid function, relieves rheumatism symptoms.
Cooking time approx. 5 min
Allergens: AFM
1 portion to 260g. / 802kcal. - (carb:21% / prot:79%)
100g.=308,46kcal. / protein 22,11g. fat:52,97g.
µg. - Ph:138,82 Na:313,1 Ka:257,72 Mg:28,88 Ca:84,62 Fe:0,54 Zn:0,48 Col.:0,06
Hsr.:14,65

Quantity of ingredients:
Leaf salads (bitter) 2 portions / 60g. (rec.)
Fresh cheese from soya 3/8 lbs - 6oz / 150g. (yes)
Mustard 1 knife tip / 1g. (yes)
Lemon juice 1 dash / 3g. (yes)
Salt 1 pinch / 1g. (little)
Pepper (ground) 1 pinch / 0,5g. ()
Herbs various 2 teaspoons / 4g. (yes)
Black caraway 1 pinch / 1g. (yes)
Whole grain bread 2 slices / 40g. (yes)

Cooking instructions:
Wash lettuce and finely pluck.
Mix 150 ml cream cheese, splashes of mustard, splashes of lemon juice, 1 clove of garlic, chopped fresh herbs, pinch of pepper and crushed black cumin and pour over. Serve with wholemeal bread.

9.36 Mango banana yoghurt drink ice cold

Good to fight loss of appetite, oral mucosa inflammation. Regulates gastrointestinal function, chronic constipation. Prevents cancer. Diuretic, forcing spleen.
Cooking time approx. 5 min
Allergens: G
2 portions to 226g. / 121kcal. - (carb:87% / prot:13%)
100g.=53,54kcal. / protein 2,72g. fat:1,05g.
µg. - Ph:7,97 Na:3,73 Ka:51,04 Mg:5,37 Ca:11,04 Fe:0,07 Zn:0,04 Col.:0,28 Hsr.:2,87

Quantity of ingredients:
Mango juice 1/2 cup / 100g. (little)
Yogurt (natural, 1.5% fat) 1/4 lbs - 4oz / 100g. (yes)
Mineral water 1/2 cup / 100g. (yes)
Banana 1/2 piece / 150g. (yes)
Acerola fruit nectar or powder 1 teaspoon / 2g. (little)

Cooking instructions:
Mix all the ingredients and 2-3 ice cubes in a blender.

9.37 Melanzani with olive oil and turmeric

improves blood circulation, reduces inflammation, relieves pain,
promotes digestion, helps to digest fat, supports urination, reduces
blood pressure.
Cooking time approx. 30 min
Allergens: A
2 portions to 321,5g. / 432kcal. - (carb:47% / prot:53%)
100g.=134,37kcal. / protein 6,13g. fat:30,66g.
µg. - Ph:6,14 Na:10,38 Ka:42,8 Mg:2,74 Ca:3,55 Fe:0,09 Zn:0,05 Col.:0,02 Hsr.:4,84

Quantity of ingredients:
Aubergine 2 pieces / 300g. (yes)
Olive oil 4 table spoons / 60g. (yes)
Tomato 4 pieces / 200g. (yes)
Turmeric (yellow root) 1/2 teaspoon / 1g. (yes)
Ground 1 pinch / 1g. (yes)
Salt 1 pinch / 1g. (little)
White bread (wheat bread) 4 slices / 80g. (little)

Cooking instructions:
Cut the Melanzani into slices and spread them with the tomatoes on a
baking tray. Sprinkle with olive oil and then with turmeric, caraway and
salt. Bake them in the tube 20 min.
Serve with the white bread.

9.38 Millet with pears

Refreshing and nourishing, promotes digestion, supports urination, good to fight cough, promotes perspiration, reduces blood lipids, stimulates, dissolves stagnation, forces liver, strengthens the muscles, lowers cholesterol, antiparasitic.
Cooking time approx. 35 min
Allergens: G
5 portions to 238,4g. / 213kcal. - (carb:86% / prot:14%)
100g.=89,43kcal. / protein 3,91g. fat:3,24g.
µg. - Ph:1,89 Na:0,11 Ka:4,29 Mg:0,99 Ca:0,53 Fe:0,05 Zn:0,02 Col.:0 Hsr.:0,77

Quantity of ingredients:
Millet 1 cup / 120g. (yes)
Water 1 1/2 cups / 200g. (yes)
Grape juice red 1 1/2 cups / 240g. (yes)
Pear 4 pieces / 600g. (yes)
Ginger fresh 1/2 teaspoon / 2g. (yes)
Salt 1 pinch / 1g. (little)
Acerola fruit nectar or powder 1 teaspoon / 2g. (little)
Cocoa 1 pinch / 1g. (rec.)
Sunflower seeds 2 table spoons / 4g. (yes)
Barley malt 1/2 teaspoon / 2g. (yes)
Cream, sweet 30% 2 teaspoons / 20g. (little)

Cooking instructions:
Simmer the millet for 5 min and let it swell for another 30 min.

Then: In a hot pot, heat some grape juice; add chopped pears, very little grated ginger, a pinch of salt, acerola, a pinch of cocoa and sauté briefly; add the boiled millet, sunflower seeds, some barley malt to taste, 1 tsp cream per serving or a little butter.

9.39 Noodles with vegetable and tomato sauce

Protects the digestive system. Detoxifying, Good to fight loss of appetite, flatulence, inflammatory bowel disease, obesity, gout, stomach ulcers, stomach cramps, rheumatism, heartburn, twelffinger intestinal ulcers, promotes digestion, helps to digest fat.
Cooking time approx. 45 min
Allergens: ACG
2 portions to 281g. / 562kcal. - (carb:70% / prot:30%)
100g.=199,82kcal. / protein 14,06g. fat:21,68g.
µg. - Ph:21,13 Na:3,21 Ka:44,61 Mg:8,06 Ca:6,77 Fe:0,3 Zn:0,2 Col.:8,37 Hsr.:18,02

Quantity of ingredients:
Tomato 1/4 lbs - 4oz / 125g. (yes)
Carrot 1 piece / 80g. (yes)
Zucchini 1 piece / 80g. (yes)
Olive oil 1 table spoon / 15g. (yes)
Onion (shallot) 1 piece / 20g. (yes)
Oregano dried 1 pinch / 1g. (yes)
Salt 1 pinch / 1g. (little)
Pepper (ground) 1 pinch / 0,2g. ()
Noodles (wheat) with egg 5/8 oz / 200g. (yes)
Olive oil 1 table spoon / 10g. (yes)
Crème fraiche cheese 2 table spoons / 30g. (little)

Cooking instructions:
Boil the tomatoes with a little water, drain and collect the juice, cut the tomatoes into pieces.
Roughly grate zucchini and carrot. Heat olive oil in a pot. Steam shallots very soft. Add tomatoes, season with oregano, salt and pepper. Simmer tomatoes to a thick sauce.
Bring plenty of salted water to boil, cook the wholegrain noodles until firm. In the cooking time of the pasta, heat in a pan olive oil. Fry the carrots while stirring, lightly salt. Add zucchini, sauté briefly while stirring. The vegetables should be soft with a bite.
Drain pasta, mix with crème fraiche, season with salt and pepper. Garnish with the tomato sauce.

9.40 Oat Congee

Strengthens immune system.
Cooking time approx. 2-4 hours
Allergens: A
3 portions to 275g. / 162kcal. - (carb:74% / prot:26%)
100g.=58,91kcal. / protein 7,04g. fat:2,87g.
µg. - Ph:5,76 Na:0,23 Ka:5,98 Mg:2,27 Ca:1,82 Fe:0,1 Zn:0,08 Col.:0 Hsr.:2,51

Quantity of ingredients:
Oat 1 cup / 125g. (yes)
Water 6 cups / 700g. (yes)

Cooking instructions:
Cook oats and water in a ratio of about 1: 6. The amount of water determines the thickness of the mash (pure matter of taste). The oats swell, so do not take much. Put the oats in a saucepan with good insulation and a heavy lid. It is important to simmer the oats after a

short boil on the slightest flame, otherwise it burns. Cook the oat for 2-4 hours. The longer it cooks, the more he strengthens.

9.41 Oriental rice pan

Forcing spleen, dissolves stagnation, promotes weight loss. Good to fight immunodeficiency, loss of appetite, flatulence. Numerous vitamins, minerals and secondary plant active ingredients.
Cooking time approx. 30 min
Allergens: EL
6 portions to 271,83g. / 303kcal. - (carb:81% / prot:19%)
100g.=111,47kcal. / protein 9,51g. fat:5,44g.
µg. - Ph:2,35 Na:0,71 Ka:4,97 Mg:1,97 Ca:4,24 Fe:0,03 Zn:0,01 Col.:0 Hsr.:2,04

Quantity of ingredients:
Rice (whole grain) 3/8 lbs - 6oz / 180g. (yes)
Basic recipe for a vegetable soup (nutritious) 2 1/4 cups / 500g. (yes)
Curry 1/2 teaspoon / 2g. (yes)
Onion (spring onion) 4 pieces / 80g. (yes)
Rapeseed oil 2 table spoons / 20g. (yes)
Peppers 1/4 lbs - 4oz / 120g. (yes)
Corn 3 oz / 80g. (yes)
Shiitake, dried 1/2 oz / 80g. (yes)
Bamboo shoots 3 oz / 80g. (yes)
Peas 3 oz / 80g. (yes)
Peaches 1/8 lbs - 2oz / 60g. (yes)
Pineapple 1/8 lbs - 2oz / 60g. (yes)
Tomato 5/8 oz / 200g. (yes)
Lovage 1 teaspoon / 2g. (yes)
Basil (fresh) 1 teaspoon / 2g. (yes)
Parsley 1 teaspoon / 2g. (yes)
Lemon Balm (fresh) 1 teaspoon / 2g. (yes)
Pepper (ground) 1 pinch / 1g. ()

Cooking instructions:
Soak the mushrooms in water 20 min.
Boil the rice in the vegetable stock 15 min. and season with some curry.
Peel the onion, cut into fine cubes.
Heat the oil in a pan and sauté the onion cubes.
Wash the peppers in half, remove the core, cut into cubes and add.
Add corn, mushrooms and bamboo shoots, simmer 5 min. until firm.
Also add the bean sprouts, peas, peach cubes and pineapple cubes.
Then add the peeled, chopped tomatoes.
Add the cooked rice and season with the herbs and pepper.

9.42 Pancakes with spinach and parmesan

Promotes bowel movement, improves blood circulation, forcing spleen and bowel, strengthens immune system, good to fight loss of appetite, flatulence, high blood pressure, depressions, diabetes, constipation, inflammatory bowel disease
Cooking time approx. 25 min
Allergens: ACGL
6 portions to 303g. / 330kcal. - (carb:46% / prot:54%)
100g.=108,8kcal. / protein 17,5g. fat:18,52g.
µg. - Ph:3,27 Na:3,24 Ka:6,47 Mg:0,96 Ca:4,52 Fe:0,05 Zn:0,02 Col.:1,32 Hsr.:1,02

Quantity of ingredients:
Wholemeal flour 1/4 lbs - 4oz / 100g. (yes)
Wheat flour 1/4 lbs - 4oz / 100g. (yes)
Chicken egg 4 pieces / 200g. (yes)
Cow's milk (whole milk 3.5% fat) 1 1/2 cups / 400g. (yes)
Salt 1 pinch / 1g. (little)
Sunflower oil 1 table spoon / 15g. (yes)
Olive oil 1 table spoon / 15g. (yes)
Onion white 1 piece / 50g. (yes)
Parsley 1/2 bunch / 80g. (yes)
Basic recipe for a vegetable soup (nutritious) 1/2 cup / 150g. (yes)
Basil (fresh) 1/4 teaspoon / 1g. (yes)
Nutmeg 1 pinch / 0,3g. (yes)
Crème fraiche cheese 3 table spoons / 45g. (little)
Spinach 1,3 lbs / 600g. (yes)
Salt 1 pinch / 1g. (little)
Pepper (ground) 1 pinch / 0,1g. ()
Parmesan 1/8 lbs - 2oz / 60g. (little)

Cooking instructions:
Stir flour, eggs and milk and a pinch of salt with the whisk until smooth. From the dough, fry pancakes crispy brown on both sides.

Heat oil in a small saucepan. Fry the finely chopped onion until tender. Stir in chopped parsley, sauté briefly. Add the vegetable broth according to the basic recipe, season with basil and nutmeg. Cover and simmer for 15 minutes, add creme fraiche and finely puree.
Cook the washed, drizzled spinach with a little salt in a closed pan over a moderate heat in 3 minutes, drain in a sieve and cut into small pieces. Add the spinach to the sauce, heat briefly. Add parmesan in the mix. Fill the pancakes with the cream spinach.

9.43 Paprika-tomato rice

Good to fight little cholesterol, diabetes. Low in protein, low fat content, little protein. Forcing spleen, dissolves stagnation, promotes weight loss. Good to fight immunodeficiency, loss of appetite, flatulence, high blood pressure, depressions.
Cooking time approx. 25 min
Allergens: L
3 portions to 324g. / 291kcal. - (carb:89% / prot:11%)
100g.=89,92kcal. / protein 7,63g. fat:2,54g.
µg. - Ph:10,3 Na:1,31 Ka:15,5 Mg:9,5 Ca:22,5 Fe:0,14 Zn:0,06 Col.:0 Hsr.:4,12

Quantity of ingredients:
Onion white 1 piece / 50g. (yes)
Peppers 4 pieces / 120g. (yes)
Bay leaf 2 pieces / 1g. (yes)
Clove 2 pieces / 1g. (yes)
Basic recipe for a vegetable soup (nutritious) 7/8 lbs / 400g. (yes)
Rice (whole grain) 5/8 oz / 200g. (yes)
Champignon 1/8 lbs - 2oz / 60g. (yes)
Parsley 1/2 oz / 20g. (yes)
Pepper (ground) 1 pinch / 0,2g. ()
Peppers (rose peppers) 1 pinch / 0,2g. (yes)
Tomato 1/4 lbs - 4oz / 120g. (yes)

Cooking instructions:
Finely chop the onion. Cut the peppers into fine strips.
Heat margarine in a saucepan, sauté onions and peppers, and rice.
Add the vegetable stock, add cloves and bay leaves and leave to simmer in a closed pot for approx. 20 minutes. Cut the tomato meat into 1 cm cubes and add to the rice 5 minutes before the end of cooking.

9.44 Parsley cream sauce

Reduces blood pressure, strengthens immune system, forcing spleen, dissolves stagnation, improves digestion, lowers cholesterol. Stimulates liver function, detoxifying.
Cooking time approx. 25 min
Allergens: GL
2 portions to 234g. / 118kcal. - (carb:81% / prot:19%)
100g.=50,64kcal. / protein 2,91g. fat:5,51g.
µg. - Ph:9,31 Na:4,41 Ka:34,59 Mg:20,78 Ca:79,47 Fe:0,2 Zn:0,07 Col.:1,12 Hsr.:1,84

Quantity of ingredients:
Basic recipe for a vegetable soup (nutritious) 3/4 lbs / 300g. (yes)
Potato 1/4 lbs - 4oz / 100g. (yes)
Parsley 1 Bunch / 15g. (yes)
Nutmeg 1 pinch / 0,5g. (yes)
Coriander 1/2 teaspoon / 1g. (yes)
Sour cream 15% fat 1/8 lbs - 2oz / 50g. (little)
Fennel seeds ground 1/2 teaspoon / 1g. (yes)
Ginger powder 1 pinch / 0,5g. (yes)

Cooking instructions:
Broth the vegetables soup according to the basic recipe with peeled, diced potatoes, half of the finely chopped parsley and nutmeg. Cover and simmer until the potatoes are tender.

Using the blender, puree the vegetable broth, potatoes, remaining freshly chopped parsley, fennel, ginger and sour cream into a smooth sauce.

9.45 Pear compote

Promotes digestion, supports urination.
Cooking time approx. 20 min
3 portions to 246,67g. / 100kcal. - (carb:93% / prot:7%)
100g.=40,54kcal. / protein 1g. fat:0,66g.
µg. - Ph:1,13 Na:0,19 Ka:9,38 Mg:0,56 Ca:0,86 Fe:0,02 Zn:0,02 Col.:0 Hsr.:1,13

Quantity of ingredients:
Water 1 1/2 cups / 240g. (yes)
Pear 4 / 500g. (yes)

Cooking instructions:
Halve organic pears. Cores and skin can be used. Pear in the pot and add water. Simmer for up to 20 minutes until pears are tender.

9.46 Pear juice

Promotes digestion, supports urination.
Cooking time approx. 5 min
2 portions to 300g. / 180kcal. - (carb:93% / prot:7%)
100g.=60kcal. / protein 1,8g. fat:1,2g.
µg. - Ph:7,5 Na:1 Ka:62,5 Mg:3,5 Ca:4,5 Fe:0,15 Zn:0,05 Col.:0 Hsr.:7,5

Quantity of ingredients:
Pear 3 pieces / 600g. (yes)

Cooking instructions:
Peel pears thinly (vitamins under the skin) and core. Juice in the juicer.

9.47 Polenta with peach

Relieves fatigue, forcing spleen, diuretic, strengthens the defense, good to fight fungi infections, lets urine and bile juice flow, prevents the aging process, strengthens brain cells.
Cooking time approx. 20 min
3 portions to 254g. / 197kcal. - (carb:89% / prot:11%)
100g.=77,56kcal. / protein 4,48g. fat:0,6g.
µg. - Ph:2,76 Na:0,12 Ka:11,83 Mg:0,93 Ca:1,02 Fe:0,05 Zn:0,02 Col.:0 Hsr.:1,56

Quantity of ingredients:
Water 1 1/2 cups / 240g. (yes)
Corn Grease (Polenta) 1 cup / 120g. (yes)
Peaches 2-3 pieces / 400g. (yes)
Vanilla pod 1 pinch / 1g. (yes)
Chili (pod or ground) 1 pinch / 0,1g. (yes)
Cinnamon ground 1 pinch / 1g. (yes)

Cooking instructions:
Pour the polenta into a pan of hot water with constant stirring until the polenta has the desired consistency. Pull the
polenta from the fire and let it soak for 10 minutes.

Wash fresh peaches and cut into quarters. Pour into the finished polenta the peaches, add the vanilla and add Chili to taste, stir and let it go for 3 minutes.

Winter varieties: Pickled fruit, pear, apples

9.48 Porridge with raisins and sake

Strengthens immune system, improves blood circulation, improves medication effect, stimulates appetite, detoxifies the skin, stimulates nerves, frees breathing, increases body temperature, promotes perspiration.
Cooking time approx. 10 min
Allergens: AGO
1 portion to 356g. / 427kcal. - (carb:67% / prot:33%)
100g.=119,94kcal. / protein 11,78g. fat:16,8g.
µg. - Ph:107,91 Na:22,97 Ka:150,88 Mg:29,72 Ca:60,08 Fe:0,83 Zn:0,87 Col.:2,11 Hsr.:25,96

Quantity of ingredients:
Oat flakes (whole grain) 8 table spoons / 60g. (yes)
Water 1/2 cup / 125g. (yes)
Cow's milk (whole milk 3.5% fat) 1/2 cup / 125g. (yes)
Salt 1 pinch / 1g. (little)
Cream, sweet 30% 2 table spoons / 20g. (little)
Raisins 1 table spoon / 15g. (little)
Sake 1 table spoon / 10g. (yes)

Cooking instructions:
Heat water and milk and a pinch of salt till it boils. Sprinkle in 4 tablespoons of coarse rolled oats and cook to a pulp, add 4 tablespoons of fine oatmeal, allow to simmer. Arrange in a preheated bowl and top with cream.
Add raisins and sake.

9.49 Potato gnocchi with vegetables and basil sauce

Strengthens immune system, promotes weight loss. Good to fight immunodeficiency, loss of appetite, flatulence, high blood pressure. Relaxing and reassuring.
Cooking time approx. 1 hour
Allergens: ACGL
4 portions to 290,25g. / 167kcal. - (carb:75% / prot:25%)
100g.=57,45kcal. / protein 6,54g. fat:4,63g.
µg. - Ph:3,26 Na:1,11 Ka:13,57 Mg:2,45 Ca:9,39 Fe:0,06 Zn:0,02 Col.:1,36 Hsr.:1,49

Quantity of ingredients:
Potato 5/8 lbs - 8oz / 250g. (yes)
Wheat flour 1 oz / 25g. (yes)

Wheat semolina 1/2 oz / 15g. (yes)
Chicken yolk 1 piece / 20g. (yes)
Nutmeg 1 pinch / 0,2g. (yes)
Basic recipe for a vegetable soup (nutritious) 1 cup / 250g. (yes)
Celery root 1/8 lbs - 2oz / 50g. (yes)
Lemon peel 1/2 teaspoon / 2g. (yes)
Ginger fresh 1/2 teaspoon / 2g. (yes)
Nutmeg 1 pinch / 0,2g. (yes)
Basil (fresh) 1 Bunch / 125g. (yes)
Crème fraiche cheese 1 table spoon / 20g. (little)
Salt 1 pinch / 1g. (little)
Pepper (ground) 1 pinch / 0,2g. ()
Carrot 1/4 lbs - 4oz / 100g. (yes)
Zucchini 1/4 lbs - 4oz / 100g. (yes)
Cauliflower 1/4 lbs - 4oz / 100g. (yes)
Broccoli 1/4 lbs - 4oz / 100g. (yes)
Salt 1 pinch / 1g. (little)

Cooking instructions:
Steam the potatoes gently, peel and pass hot through the potato press.
Process the hot potatoes with flour, semolina, egg, nutmeg and salt to a
smooth dough. Let dough rest for 3o minutes.
Make small rolls (2 cm) out of the dough with flour-dusted hands, cut off
1 cm thin slices. To create the typical gnocchi shape, gently dab the
dough pieces with your thumb. Leave the gnocchi in lightly boiling
salted water for 6 - 8 minutes. Lift the gnocchi out of the pot with the
skimmer.

Heat the vegetable stock till it boils. Add diced celery, grated lemon
peel, finely chopped ginger and 1 pinch of nutmeg. Cover and simmer
for about 10 minutes. Using the blender, puree the vegetable broth,
celery, chopped basil and crème fraiche into a smooth sauce. Season
with salt and nutmeg.

Cut carrots, zucchini, cauliflower and broccoli into small pieces and
cook covered in a sieve over steam for 8 minutes until firm.
Heat the sauce again and add to the vegetables and arrange over the
gnocchi.

9.50 Pumpkin-yoghurt soup

Relaxes, reduces blood pressure, strengthens immune system, promotes weight loss. Good to fight immunodeficiency, loss of appetite, flatulence, depressions, diabetes, diarrhea.
Cooking time approx. 15 min
Allergens: GL
4 portions to 239g. / 68kcal. - (carb:83% / prot:17%)
100g.=28,45kcal. / protein 2,37g. fat:1,31g.
µg. - Ph:1,79 Na:0,9 Ka:6,6 Mg:2,8 Ca:10,96 Fe:0,02 Zn:0,01 Col.:0,05 Hsr.:0,35

Quantity of ingredients:
Basic recipe for a vegetable soup (nutritious) 1 cup / 300g. (yes)
Hokkaido pumpkin 1,1 lbs / 500g. (yes)
Ginger fresh 1/2 teaspoon / 2g. (yes)
Fennel seeds ground 1/2 teaspoon / 1g. (yes)
Anise (Common Fennel) 1/4 teaspoon / 1g. (yes)
Yogurt (natural, 1.5% fat) 3/8 lbs - 6oz / 150g. (yes)
Peppermint 2 leaves / 1g. (yes)
Salt 1 pinch / 1g. (little)

Cooking instructions:
Heat the vegetable broth (after the basic recipe) till it boils. Add diced pumpkin, chopped ginger, crushed fennel seeds and anise. Bring the soup to the boil and simmer for about 12 minutes until the pumpkin is soft.
Remove soup from the heat. Puree the soup with the yoghurt with the blender. Serve soup with finely chopped mint sprinkled.

9.51 Mashed banana

Eat 2 times a day, regulates gastrointestinal function
Cooking time approx. 7 min
1 portion to 150g. / 144kcal. - (carb:95% / prot:5%)
100g.=96kcal. / protein 1,65g. fat:0,3g.
µg. - Ph:28 Na:1 Ka:393 Mg:36 Ca:9 Fe:0,6 Zn:0,2 Col.:0 Hsr.:25

Quantity of ingredients:
Banana 1 piece / 150g. (yes)

Cooking instructions:
Mix the banana with the fork or purée with a blender. Leave to brown for at least 5 minutes.

9.52 Quick zucchini soup

Diuretic, supports urination. Strengthens gastrointestinal function, expands blood vessels, prevents cancer, prevents diseases (in the elderly). Stimulates liver function, detoxifying.
Cooking time approx. 10 min
4 portions to 241,5g. / 42kcal. - (carb:46% / prot:54%)
100g.=17,29kcal. / protein 1,76g. fat:2,04g.
µg. - Ph:3,81 Na:0,41 Ka:29,78 Mg:3,2 Ca:5,37 Fe:0,21 Zn:0,01 Col.:0 Hsr.:2,85

Quantity of ingredients:
Zucchini 2-3 pieces / 500g. (yes)
Onion white 1 piece / 50g. (yes)
Corn germ oil 2 table spoons / 6g. (yes)
Parsley 1 table spoon / 7g. (yes)
Chives 1 teaspoon / 3g. (yes)
Water 2 cup / 400g. (yes)

Cooking instructions:
Fry chopped onion in oil. Add sliced zucchini and sauté well. Pour with water. Chop parsley and chives, add and puree everything.

9.53 Rice congee with chicken liver and buckthorn fruit

Good to fight blood circulation disorders, thrombose, risk of embolism, high blood pressure, a headache, heart attack and stroke. Has many vitamins and minerals, high quality amino acid profile. Regulates the blood pressure and blood glucose level, forcing spleen.
Cooking time approx. 3 hours
Allergens: EO
3 portions to 307,67g. / 176kcal. - (carb:94% / prot:6%)
100g.=57,1kcal. / protein 7,51g. fat:1,45g.
µg. - Ph:4,49 Na:2,71 Ka:4,23 Mg:29,58 Ca:28,04 Fe:0,08 Zn:0,05 Col.:1,44 Hsr.:2,41

Quantity of ingredients:
Basic recipe for a rice soup (Congee) 5 cups / 800g. (yes)
Chicken liver 1/2 cup / 60g. (little)
Bocksdorn fruits (Fructus Lycii, goji berry dried 1/2 cup / 60g. (yes)
Soy sauce 1 dash / 3g. (yes)

Cooking instructions:
Cook basic recipe for rice congee with the chicken liver and wolfberry fruits; Season with soy sauce.

9.54 Rice congee with honey pear and black sesame

Promotes digestion, supports urination, good to fight blood circulation disorders, thromboses, risk of embolism, high blood pressure, a headache, heart attack and stroke.
Cooking time approx. 10 min - 3 hours
Allergens: N
2 portions to 271,5g. / 158kcal. - (carb:95% / prot:5%)
100g.=58,38kcal. / protein 2,43g. fat:1,55g.
µg. - Ph:4,8 Na:0,43 Ka:18,44 Mg:35,15 Ca:34,31 Fe:0,09 Zn:0,06 Col.:0 Hsr.:2,88

Quantity of ingredients:
Basic recipe for a rice soup (Congee) 1 1/2 cups / 240g. (yes)
Pear 2 pieces / 300g. (yes)
Sesame, black 1 teaspoon / 3g. (yes)

Cooking instructions:
Cook rice congee according to basic recipe.
Fill pot with 3 cm of water and heat till it boils. Quarter the pears (with the skin and seeds) and simmer them covered with black sesame for 10 minutes. Mix with the rice.

9.55 Rice with stewed vegetables

Reduces blood pressure, strengthens immune system, prevents cancer, reduces radiation damage, extremely low fat content, good to fight blood circulation disorders, thrombose, risk of embolism, a headache, heart attack and stroke. Is diuretic.
Cooking time approx. 20 min
Allergens: L
2 portions to 310,5g. / 166kcal. - (carb:82% / prot:18%)
100g.=53,62kcal. / protein 4,33g. fat:2,25g.
µg. - Ph:8,31 Na:2,83 Ka:26,32 Mg:3,14 Ca:5,9 Fe:0,2 Zn:0,07 Col.:0 Hsr.:6,32

Quantity of ingredients:
Rice variety any 1/2 cup / 60g. (yes)
Water 3 cups / 300g. (yes)
Lemon peel 1 piece / 3g. (yes)
Water 1/2 cup / 0g. (yes)
Carrot 2 pieces / 180g. (yes)
Celery sticks 1/2 piece / 5g. (yes)
Champignon 1/2 cup / 50g. (yes)
Cress 2 table spoons / 20g. (yes)
Linseed oil 1 dash / 3g. (yes)

Cooking instructions:
Cook rice according to basic recipe with a piece of lemon peel.
Steam chopped carrots, celery and mushrooms until soft.
Then sprinkle with cress. Then add a dash of high quality cold oil.

9.56 Roasted barley patties

Improves digestion, lowers cholesterol, good to fight diarrhea,
ulceration, joint pain, stomach problems. Promotes spleen and liver,
reduces blood pressure, strengthens immune system, prevents cancer,
reduces radiation damage, stimulates liver function.
Cooking time approx. 1 1/2 hours
Allergens: ACN
3 portions to 292,67g. / 398kcal. - (carb:63% / prot:37%)
100g.=135,99kcal. / protein 8,38g. fat:19,69g.
µg. - Ph:7,07 Na:4,18 Ka:17,24 Mg:2,02 Ca:2,5 Fe:0,08 Zn:0,04 Col.:2,76 Hsr.:2,93

Quantity of ingredients:
Water 1 1/2 cups / 250g. (yes)
Barley grouts 1 cup / 120g. (yes)
Potato 1 piece / 140g. (yes)
Carrot 1 piece / 120g. (yes)
Champignon 2-3 pieces / 25g. (yes)
Chicken egg 1 piece / 55g. (yes)
Onion white 1 piece / 50g. (yes)
Ginger fresh 1/2 teaspoon / 1g. (yes)
Pepper (ground) 1 pinch / 0,5g. ()
Salt 1 pinch / 1g. (little)
Lemon 1/2 piece / 15g. (yes)
Parsley 2 table spoons / 15g. (yes)
Peppers powder 1 pinch / 1g. (yes)
Sesame oil 2 table spoons / 50g. (yes)
Bread roll 1 piece / 35g. (little)

Cooking instructions:
Preparation:
Place 2 large cups of hot water in a saucepan; add 1 large cup of barley
porridge; simmer for 2 minutes while stirring; then let it swell for 20
minutes on the switched off stove; take down and let cool.
Cook in boiling water 1 large potato, chopped and cut.
Soak 1 roll in hot water and squeeze well.
Then: Mix the barley groats and crushed the potato. Add 1 grated
carrot, 2 - 3 chopped mushrooms, 1 egg, 1 finely chopped onion, 1/2
teaspoon grated ginger, a pinch of pepper, a pinch of salt, a little lemon

juice, chopped parsley,
plenty of rose paprika; knead well and form patties; heat sesame oil in a hot pan; fry the patties for about 15 minutes over a gentle heat; turn at half time.
Also fits well: lettuce, soybean vegetables.

9.57 Roasted millet with Celery sticks

Promotes spleen and kidney, diuretic, promoting metabolism.
Cooking time approx. 30 min
Allergens: L
2 portions to 228g. / 400kcal. - (carb:82% / prot:18%)
100g.=175,44kcal. / protein 7g. fat:2,58g.
µg. - Ph:22,21 Na:4,29 Ka:15,63 Mg:11,94 Ca:5,5 Fe:0,62 Zn:0,24 Col.:0 Hsr.:6,31

Quantity of ingredients:
Millet 1 cup / 120g. (yes)
Water 1 1/2 cups / 240g. (yes)
Celery sticks 2 rods / 50g. (yes)
Water 2 table spoons / 30g. (yes)
Herbs various 1 table spoon / 10g. (yes)
Salt 1 pinch / 1g. (little)
Sage 3-4 leaves / 2g. (yes)
Cress 1 teaspoon / 3g. (yes)

Cooking instructions:
Roast millet briefly, pour over water, heat till it boils and let stand for 20 min. to swell.
Cut celery into small pieces and mix with water, salt and fresh herbs and cook for 10 min. Add to the millet. Sprinkle fresh sage or watercress over it.

9.58 Roasted millet with plum compote

Supports urination, promotes spleen and kidney, strengthens the defense. Good to fight fungi infections.
Cooking time approx. 30 min
4 portions to 218,25g. / 139kcal. - (carb:85% / prot:15%)
100g.=63,8kcal. / protein 3,57g. fat:1,24g.
µg. - Ph:2,99 Na:0,1 Ka:4,37 Mg:1,68 Ca:0,78 Fe:0,09 Zn:0,03 Col.:0 Hsr.:0,93

Quantity of ingredients:
Millet 1 cup / 120g. (yes)
Water 1 1/2 cups / 250g. (yes)
Plum 1 1/2 cups / 250g. (yes)

Vanilla pod 1 pinch / 1g. (yes)
Water 5/8 lbs - 8oz / 250g. (yes)
Cinnamon ground 1 pinch / 1g. (yes)
Acerola fruit nectar or powder 1/2 teaspoon / 1g. (little)

Cooking instructions:
Roast millet briefly, pour over water, heat till it boils and let stand for 20 min. to swell.
Cook plums with water, vanilla and cinnamon 10 min. then strain. Add acerola and add to the millet.

9.59 Rosemary Potatoes

Reduces Inflammation, improves digestion, regenerates skin, supports urination, lowers cholesterol. Rosemary stimulates digestion, strengthens lung, promotes spleen and kidney, dries out.
Cooking time approx. 30 min
2 portions to 216,5g. / 188kcal. - (carb:76% / prot:24%)
100g.=87,07kcal. / protein 4,21g. fat:5,25g.
µg. - Ph:11,51 Na:0,72 Ka:82,88 Mg:4,72 Ca:1,86 Fe:0,1 Zn:0,07 Col.:0 Hsr.:3,64

Quantity of ingredients:
Potato 6-8 pieces / 420g. (yes)
Salt (herbal) 1 pinch / 1g. (little)
Olive oil 1 table spoon / 10g. (yes)
Rosemary 1 teaspoon / 2g. (yes)

Cooking instructions:
Cut the potatoes into half´s, apply a little olive oil on the cut surface, then salt, sprinkle 2 - 3 rosemary needles on the potatoes.
Place the potatoes on the baking tray and bake them in the preheated oven for approx. 25 minutes to 190°C/374°F.

9.60 Scrambled eggs with leaf salad olives and tomatoes

Calms nerves and stomach, relieves fatigue, regulates gastrointestinal function, promotes digestion, stimulates liver function, detoxifying, helps to digest fat, supports urination, reduces blood pressure.
Cooking time approx. 10 min
Allergens: C
1 portion to 264g. / 419kcal. - (carb:8% / prot:92%)
100g.=158,71kcal. / protein 24,4g. fat:33,87g.
µg. - Ph:158,54 Na:226,49 Ka:184,78 Mg:13,81 Ca:53,55 Fe:1,72 Zn:1,03 Col.:270,04 Hsr.:7,46

Quantity of ingredients:
Chicken egg 2-3 pieces / 180g. (yes)
Olive oil 1 table spoon / 10g. (yes)
Salt 1 pinch / 1g. (little)
Pepper (ground) 1 pinch / 0,5g. ()
Olives 6 pieces / 10g. (yes)
Tomato 1 piece / 50g. (yes)
Lettuce 2 leaves / 5g. (rec.)
Turmeric (yellow root) 1 pinch / 1g. (yes)
Parsley 1/2 teaspoon / 5g. (yes)
Basil (fresh) 2-3 leaves / 2g. (yes)

Cooking instructions:
Heat olive oil in the pan. Cut the tomato into a slice. Pluck salad into small pieces. Briefly fry tomatoes, lettuce and olives. Meanwhile mix eggs with salt and spices with a fork.
Pour the egg and spices into the pan. Stir with a wooden spoon until it reaches the desired consistency.
Spices and herbs: turmeric, parsley, basil, black cumin

9.61 Semolina soup with vegetables

Reduces blood pressure, strengthens immune system, prevents cancer, forcing spleen, dissolves stagnation, promotes weight loss. Good to fight immunodeficiency, loss of appetite, flatulence, high blood pressure, depressions, diabetes, diarrhea, rheumatism, heartburn, twelffinger intestinal ulcers.
Cooking time approx. 20 min
Allergens: AGL
3 portions to 237,67g. / 105kcal. - (carb:85% / prot:15%)
100g.=44,32kcal. / protein 2,38g. fat:4,24g.
µg. - Ph:2,88 Na:3,04 Ka:8,54 Mg:9,5 Ca:37,49 Fe:0,11 Zn:0,03 Col.:0 Hsr.:1,7

Quantity of ingredients:
Basic recipe for a vegetable soup (nutritious) 2 cup / 500g. (yes)
Wheat semolina 2 table spoons / 20g. (yes)
Lovage 1/2 teaspoon / 2g. (yes)
Basil (fresh) 1/2 teaspoon / 1g. (yes)
Nutmeg 1 pinch / 0,1g. (yes)
Carrot 1/4 lbs - 4oz / 100g. (yes)
Celery root 1/8 lbs - 2oz / 50g. (yes)
Cream, sweet 30% 3 table spoons / 30g. (little)
Parsley 1 table spoon / 10g. (yes)

Cooking instructions:
Roast wheat grits without fat in a pan. Roast the chopped carrots and celery briefly. Add the vegetable soup (Basic recipe for a vegetable soup). Season with lovage, nutmeg and let it 10 min. simmer.
Stir in the cream before serving and garnish with parsley.

9.62 Spicy Tofu Vegetable Pan

Forcing spleen, relieves constipation, detoxifying, reduces inflammation, improves blood circulation, promotes sweating, dissolves stagnation, reduces flatulence, reduces blood pressure, strengthens immune system, prevents cancer, reduces radiation damage.
Cooking time approx. 25 min
Allergens: EN
4 portions to 329,25g. / 241kcal. - (carb:67% / prot:33%)
100g.=73,27kcal. / protein 7,37g. fat:7,32g.
µg. - Ph:3,76 Na:4,32 Ka:9,86 Mg:2,38 Ca:3,32 Fe:0,08 Zn:0,02 Col.:0,01 Hsr.:1,82

Quantity of ingredients:
Sesame oil 2 table spoons / 20g. (yes)
Carrot 2 pieces / 100g. (yes)
Fennel 1 piece / 250g. (yes)
Leek 1 piece / 200g. (yes)
Salt 1 pinch / 1g. (little)
Turmeric (yellow root) 1 pinch / 1g. (yes)
Lemon juice 1 splash / 1g. (yes)
Soy Tofu 1 package / 120g. (yes)
Pepper (ground) 1 pinch / 0,5g. ()
Soy sauce 1 dash / 3g. (yes)
Rice (whole grain) 1 cup / 120g. (yes)
Water 6 cups / 500g. (yes)
Salt 1 pinch / 1g. (little)

Cooking instructions:
Heat sesame oil in a hot wok or a hot pan; fry the chopped carrots, fennel and leek slices; salt, a dash of lemon juice, turmeric, tofu cubes roast for 1 - 2 minutes.
Add the pepper and cook covered for about 5 minutes; drizzle with soy sauce.
Place the rice in salted water, heat till it boils and let it simmer over low heat for about 15 minutes.

9.63 Spring salad

Blood-forming, blood detoxifying, diuretic, good to fight stomach discomfort, improves digestion, diarrhea, helps to digest fat, supports urination, reduces blood pressure, detoxifying, reduces inflammation, diuretic.
Cooking time approx. 10 min
Allergens: AEMNO
4 portions to 214,25g. / 180kcal. - (carb:64% / prot:36%)
100g.=84,13kcal. / protein 7,68g. fat:5,56g.
µg. - Ph:14,38 Na:19,94 Ka:78,76 Mg:7,01 Ca:20,61 Fe:0,72 Zn:0,03 Col.:0 Hsr.:7,87

Quantity of ingredients:
Sorrel 3/8 lbs - 6oz / 150g. (yes)
Dandelion (young plants) 1/4 lbs - 4oz / 100g. (yes)
Mung bean sprouting 0,2 lbs / 75g. (yes)
Cress 1/4 lbs - 4oz / 100g. (yes)
Chives 1 Bunch / 50g. (yes)
Tomato 2 pieces / 100g. (yes)
Parsley 1 Bunch / 50g. (yes)
Sesame paste (Tahini) 2 table spoons / 16g. (yes)
Soy sauce 1 dash / 3g. (yes)
Mustard 1/2 teaspoon / 2g. (yes)
White bread (wheat bread) 6 slices / 120g. (little)
Vinegar Aceto Balsamico 1 table spoon / 8g. (yes)
Olive oil 1 table spoon / 8g. (yes)

Cooking instructions:
Wash all salad´s, mix and prepare the sauce as follows:
Mix tahini with mustard and balsamic vinegar, tamari, olive oil, chives and half of parsley. Pour the sauce over the salad and sprinkle the remaining parsley just before serving.
Serve with the white bread.

9.64 Strawberry yoghurt and almond puree mix

Relieves pain and inflammation in rheumatism. Good to fight acute or chronic constipation of the intestine. Little laxative. Relieves pain, detoxifying, bactericide.
Cooking time approx. 5 min
Allergens: GH
3 portions to 303,67g. / 134kcal. - (carb:73% / prot:27%)
100g.=44,13kcal. / protein 4,53g. fat:3,36g.
µg. - Ph:4,67 Na:1,48 Ka:16,91 Mg:1,74 Ca:5,71 Fe:0,09 Zn:0,02 Col.:0,12 Hsr.:2,16

Quantity of ingredients:
Yogurt (natural, 1.5% fat) 5/8 oz / 200g. (yes)
Strawberries 1,5 lbs / 700g. (yes)
Honey 1 teaspoon / 3g. (little)
Acerola fruit nectar or powder 1 teaspoon / 2g. (little)
Almond puree 2 teaspoons / 6g. (yes)

Cooking instructions:
Puree yoghurt, strawberries, acerola, honey and almond paste in a blender.

9.65 Tea mixture - reducing uric acid

Good to fight gout or rheumatism, joint pain, urinary tract infections, renal colic.
Cooking time approx. 10 min
2 portions to 126,5g. / 0kcal. - (carb:0% / prot:0%)
100g.=0kcal. / protein 0g. fat:0g.
µg. - Ph:0 Na:0,25 Ka:0 Mg:0,25 Ca:1,23 Fe:0 Zn:0,02 Col.:0 Hsr.:0

Quantity of ingredients:
Tea mixture uric acid lowering 2 teaspoons / 3g. (yes)
Water 1 cup / 250g. (yes)

Cooking instructions:
Get tea mixture from the pharmacy or health food store.

Brew 2 teaspoons of the mixture with 1/4 liter of boiling water, 10min. let go, strain.

Increased uric acid levels can cause joint pain at the beginning. These are a reaction to the flushing of uric acid out of the body. There should also be a lot of movement in this time in order to speed up and support the elimination process.

9.66 Tomato soup

Promotes digestion, helps to digest fat, supports urination, reduces blood pressure, dissolves stagnation. Contains unsaturated fatty acids, is antioxidative.
Cooking time approx. 10 min
2 portions to 290g. / 100kcal. - (carb:42% / prot:58%)
100g.=34,66kcal. / protein 1,78g. fat:7,9g.
µg. - Ph:4,2 Na:1,2 Ka:31,36 Mg:1,99 Ca:3,85 Fe:0,07 Zn:0,04 Col.:0,01 Hsr.:1,47

Quantity of ingredients:
Olive oil 1 table spoon / 15g. (yes)
Onion white 1 piece / 60g. (yes)
Basil (fresh) 1 teaspoon / 2g. (yes)
Cinnamon ground 1 pinch / 1g. (yes)
Pepper (ground) 1 pinch / 0,5g. ()
Salt 1 pinch / 1g. (little)
Tomato 6 pieces / 250g. (yes)
Peppers powder 1 pinch / 1g. (yes)
Water 5/8 lbs - 8oz / 250g. (yes)

Cooking instructions:
Roast the onion in a pot. Salt and spices. Briefly roast. Put washed and quartered tomatoes in the pan. Stir and sauté briefly. Add a quart of water and heat till it boils. Cook for a quarter of an hour and puree.

9.67 Tomato with mozzarella

Promotes digestion, helps to digest fat, supports urination, reduces blood pressure. Affects anorexia, good to fight flatulence, inflammatory bowel disease, bloating and nausea. Relaxing and reassuring.
Cooking time approx. 5 min
Allergens: AG
1 portion to 217g. / 436kcal. - (carb:37% / prot:63%)
100g.=200,92kcal. / protein 14,85g. fat:30,31g.
µg. - Ph:90,53 Na:176,32 Ka:158,47 Mg:12,75 Ca:109,48 Fe:0,33 Zn:0,5 Col.:10,69
Hsr.:13,46

Quantity of ingredients:
Mozzarella 1 piece / 50g. (yes)
Tomato 2 pieces / 100g. (yes)
Salt 1 pinch / 1g. (little)
Basil (fresh) 5 leaves / 6g. (yes)
Olive oil 2 table spoons / 20g. (yes)
White bread (wheat bread) 2 slices / 40g. (little)

Cooking instructions:
Cut tomatoes and mozzarella into slices. Serve with salt, basil and olive oil. Serve with white bread.

9.68 Turkey breast with vegetables (Asian)

Strengthens blood, strengthens bone marrow, dissolves stagnation, promotes digestion and is goo to fight high blood pressure. Rice to drain the body at overweight and high blood pressure.
Cooking time approx. 45 min
Allergens: AEN
2 portions to 371g. / 535kcal. - (carb:54% / prot:46%)
100g.=144,2kcal. / protein 31,92g. fat:18,02g.
µg. - Ph:27,73 Na:66,82 Ka:46,74 Mg:7,57 Ca:3,14 Fe:0,2 Zn:0,21 Col.:4,05 Hsr.:15,18

Quantity of ingredients:
Rice variety any 1 cup / 120g. (yes)
Water 6 cups / 240g. (yes)
Turkey breast meat 5/8 oz / 200g. (yes)
Ginger fresh 1/3 inch / 3g. (yes)
Garlic 1 piece / 2g. (yes)
Soy sauce 2 table spoons / 20g. (yes)
Wheat flour 2 teaspoons / 15g. (yes)
Onion (spring onion) 2 pieces / 40g. (yes)
Peppers 1/2 piece / 10g. (yes)
Champignon 8 pieces / 30g. (yes)
Sesame oil 2 table spoons / 20g. (yes)
Soy sauce 1 table spoon / 12g. (yes)
Curry 1 pinch / 2g. (yes)
Turmeric (yellow root) 1 pinch / 2g. (yes)
Chili (pod or ground) 1 pinch / 1g. (yes)
Cashews 2 teaspoons / 25g. (yes)

Cooking instructions:
Cook the rice in salted water.
Cut the turkey meat into thin strips. Peel and dice the ginger and garlic. Put together with the meat strips in a bowl. Mix 1 tbsp of soy sauce with the wheat starch and stir until smooth. Add to the meat and marinate for 30 minutes. Wash spring onions and peppers, clean and cut into small pieces. Clean and quarter the mushrooms.
Put one tablespoon of sesame oil in a pan and sauté and warm the marinated turkey. Now add the remaining oil to the pan and fry the other vegetables in it. Now add the meat and season with soy sauce and spices. Serve with the rice. Sprinkle the cashews over the dish before serving.

9.69 Turkey rolls in tomato cream

Improves digestion, lowers cholesterol, strengthens blood, strengthens bone marrow, good to fight high blood pressure,
helps to digest fat, flatulence.
Cooking time approx. 30 min
Allergens: G
2 portions to 347g. / 301kcal. - (carb:28% / prot:72%)
100g.=86,74kcal. / protein 36,9g. fat:8,02g.
µg. - Ph:27,65 Na:43,91 Ka:76,34 Mg:4,57 Ca:4,15 Fe:0,16 Zn:0,17 Col.:4,54 Hsr.:20,26

Quantity of ingredients:
Champignon 1/4 lbs - 4oz / 100g. (yes)
Turkey breast meat 5/8 oz / 200g. (yes)
Turkey ham 1/4 lbs - 4oz / 100g. (yes)
Olive oil 2 teaspoons / 6g. (yes)
Tomato 1 piece / 60g. (yes)
Cream, sweet 30% 2 table spoons / 20g. (little)
Garlic 1 piece / 2g. (yes)
Salt 1 pinch / 1g. (little)
Pepper (ground) 1 pinch / 0,5g. ()
Basil (fresh) 1 table spoon / 5g. (yes)
Potato 5/8 oz / 200g. (yes)

Cooking instructions:
Cook potatoes in salted water and peel.
Cut the turkey into schnitzel. Thoroughly clean the mushrooms, rub them and cut them into slices. Spread the mushrooms and boiled ham over the turkey schnitzel. Roll up the schnitzel, fix with a toothpick and fry in oil for about 8-10 minutes from all sides, possibly add some liquid.

Briefly dip the meat tomato in boiling water, skin, halve, remove seeds and dice the pulp. Put in the pan. Braise briefly. Add the cream to the turkey rolls and tomato pieces. Heat till it boil.

Season with garlic, salt and pepper. Serve the turkey rolls with the sauce and freshly chopped basil.

9.70 Vegetable juice

Promotes digestion, helps to digest fat, supports urination, reduces blood pressure, strengthens immune system, prevents cancer, reduces radiation damage, forcing spleen, is stimulating.
Cooking time approx. 15 min
Allergens: L
1 portion to 225g. / 64kcal. - (carb:82% / prot:18%)
100g.=28,44kcal. / protein 2,46g. fat:0,44g.
µg. - Ph:33,92 Na:30,92 Ka:205,63 Mg:13,57 Ca:34,59 Fe:1,17 Zn:0,33 Col.:0 Hsr.:19,76

Quantity of ingredients:
Celery root 1/2 oz / 20g. (yes)
Carrot 1/4 lbs - 4oz / 100g. (yes)
Tomato 1/4 lbs - 4oz / 100g. (yes)
Garlic 1 piece / 2g. (yes)
Salt 1 teaspoon / 2g. (little)
Acerola fruit nectar or powder 1/2 teaspoon / 1g. (little)

Cooking instructions:
Peel all ingredients and use the juicer to make a drink. Stir in the acerola.

9.71 Vegetable miso soup with tofu

Very powerful, strengthens after febrile illness, reduces blood pressure, strengthens immune system, prevents cancer, reduces radiation damage, improves blood circulation, strengthens liver and kidney, detoxifying, strengthens the muscles, reduces flatulence, forcing spleen.
Cooking time approx. 15 min
Allergens: EN
4 portions to 247,75g. / 107kcal. - (carb:22% / prot:78%)
100g.=43,09kcal. / protein 1,85g. fat:9,4g.
µg. - Ph:3,92 Na:13,88 Ka:10,98 Mg:1,98 Ca:4,08 Fe:0,07 Zn:0,01 Col.:0 Hsr.:1,45

Quantity of ingredients:
Sesame oil 2 table spoons / 35g. (yes)
Onion (shallot) 1 piece / 20g. (yes)
Carrot 1 piece / 70g. (yes)
Leek 2 inches / 10g. (yes)
Water 3 cups / 750g. (yes)
Endive salad 2 table spoons / 30g. (yes)

Soy Tofu 2 table spoons / 30g. (yes)
Ginger fresh 1/2 teaspoon / 1g. (yes)
Miso 2 table spoons / 15g. (yes)

Cooking instructions:
In sesame oil first sauté onions, then carrots and a little leek; Pour in water and simmer gently; add the bean sprouts and endive leaves and leave to stand; Tofu cubes, add a little ginger; at the end stir in a little cooled cooking-water the Miso.

9.72 Vegetable semolina soup

Diuretic, harmonizes the stomach and intestines, conducts bowel winds, reduces blood pressure, lowers cholesterol, detoxifying, good to fight loss of appetite, flatulence, inflammatory bowel disease, heartburn, twelffinger intestinal ulcers. Stimulates digestion, reduces pain.
Cooking time approx. 20 min
Allergens: AEGL
3 portions to 459,67g. / 199kcal. - (carb:79% / prot:21%)
100g.=43,22kcal. / protein 6,38g. fat:7,02g.
µg. - Ph:4,26 Na:4,63 Ka:23,27 Mg:6,33 Ca:22,08 Fe:0,09 Zn:0,04 Col.:0,39 Hsr.:2,88

Quantity of ingredients:
Basic recipe for a vegetable soup (nutritious) 2 cup / 500g. (yes)
Potato 1 piece / 80g. (yes)
Parsnip 1 piece / 180g. (yes)
Carrot 1 piece / 120g. (yes)
Celery root 3/8 lbs - 6oz / 150g. (yes)
Kohlrabi 1/2 piece / 200g. (yes)
Beans (green, fresh) 1/4 lbs / 100g. (yes)
Wheat semolina 2 table spoons / 24g. (yes)
Lovage 1/2 teaspoon / 2g. (yes)
Butter organic 1 table spoon / 20g. (little)
Soy sauce 1 teaspoon / 3g. (yes)

Cooking instructions:
Worm the prepared vegetable soup; cook the vegetables in the soup softly. Spread some wheatgrass and let it swell. At the end, add lovage-green and a little butter and taste with soy sauce.

9.73 Warming carrot soup

Strengthens and warms, reduces blood pressure, strengthens immune system, prevents cancer, reduces radiation damage, strengthens gastrointestinal function.
Cooking time approx. 30 min
Allergens: HL
3 portions to 274,67g. / 133kcal. - (carb:79% / prot:21%)
100g.=48,54kcal. / protein 2,16g. fat:7,86g.
µg. - Ph:2,86 Na:2,31 Ka:9,18 Mg:8,37 Ca:32,64 Fe:0,13 Zn:0,03 Col.:0 Hsr.:1

Quantity of ingredients:
Carrot 4 pieces / 250g. (yes)
Walnut oil 2 table spoons / 20g. (yes)
Onion (shallot) 2 pieces / 40g. (yes)
Anise (Common Fennel) 1/2 teaspoon / 1g. (yes)
Nutmeg 1 pinch / 1g. (yes)
Ginger fresh 1/2 teaspoon / 1g. (yes)
Salt 1 pinch / 1g. (little)
Basic recipe for a vegetable soup (nutritious) 2 cup / 500g. (yes)
Parsley 1 table spoon / 10g. (yes)

Cooking instructions:
Heat walnut oil in a hot pot and fry onions; steam the carrots in it; add anise, nutmeg, a little ginger, salt and sauté everything; add water or vegetable- or meat stock; cook everything soft and then puree; fold in parsley at the end.

Recommendation: Suitable for the cold season, especially if you use meat broth as a liquid for infusion.

9.74 Wild garlic dumplings

Improves the flow characteristics of the blood, reduces blood pressure, lowers cholesterol.
Cooking time approx. 30 min
Allergens: ACG
4 portions to 383,25g. / 906kcal. - (carb:47% / prot:53%)
100g.=236,33kcal. / protein 30,27g. fat:15,12g.
µg. - Ph:6,46 Na:14,4 Ka:15,47 Mg:1,53 Ca:4,4 Fe:0,07 Zn:0,04 Col.:1,54 Hsr.:4,23

Quantity of ingredients:
Potato (mealy) 1,1 lbs / 500g. (yes)
Wild garlic (garlic spinach) 5/8 oz / 200g. (yes)
Butter (half fat) 1/8 lbs - 2oz / 40g. (yes)
Wheat flour 3/8 lbs - 6oz / 150g. (yes)
Wheat semolina 1/8 lbs - 2oz / 50g. (yes)
Chicken yolk 2 pieces / 20g. (yes)
Onion white 1 piece / 50g. (yes)
Butter (half fat) 1/2 oz / 10g. (yes)
Tomato 5/8 oz / 200g. (yes)
Sugar white 1 pinch / 1g. (little)
Turkey ham 5/8 lbs - 8oz / 250g. (yes)
Olive oil 1 table spoon / 10g. (yes)
Parmesan 1/8 lbs - 2oz / 50g. (little)
Salt 1 pinch / 1g. (little)
Pepper (ground) 1 pinch / 0,5g. ()
Nutmeg 1 pinch / 0,5g. (yes)

Cooking instructions:
Boil potatoes in salted water, peel and squeeze through the press while still hot. Fresh wild garlic: wash, clean and briefly dive into sparkling boiling salt water (blanch). Quench cold and express. Coarsely chop the wild garlic. Dried wild garlic: Leave approx. 100g wild garlic in 100g of water for 10 minutes and use with the water.

Melt 50g of the butter. Mix flour, semolina, egg yolks and liquid butter with the potato mixture, knead in wild garlic. Season with salt and pepper and grated nutmeg and let rest for about 15 minutes.

Peel onion, finely chop and fry in the remaining butter. Add chopped tomatoes, simmer for a few minutes, season with salt and pepper and sugar.

Make 3 dumplings per person from the potato mixture. Soak in salted water for about 15 minutes.

In the meantime lightly fry the ham in oil. Rub the cheese. Drain the dumplings, serve with the ham, the tomato sauce and grated cheese.

9.75 Wild garlic pesto

Improves the flow characteristics of the blood, high vitamin C content, stomach- und blood detoxifying, good to fight arteriosclerosis, high blood pressure.
Cooking time approx. 10 min
Allergens: G
2 portions to 165,5g. / 796kcal. - (carb:4% / prot:96%)
100g.=480,66kcal. / protein 14,01g. fat:82,66g.
µg. - Ph:41,03 Na:32,27 Ka:54,31 Mg:13,21 Ca:39,5 Fe:0,65 Zn:0,29 Col.:1,95 Hsr.:1,26

Quantity of ingredients:
Wild garlic (garlic spinach) 1/4 lbs - 4oz / 125g. (yes)
Parmesan 1 oz / 30g. (little)
Pine nuts 1/8 lbs - 2oz / 50g. (yes)
Olive oil 1/4 lbs - 4oz / 125g. (yes)
Salt 1 pinch / 1g. (little)
Pepper (ground) 1 pinch / 0,3g. ()

Cooking instructions:
Fresh wild garlic: Wash the wild garlic leaves and dry them carefully. Cut the wild garlic leaves into fine strips. Dried wild garlic: Leave approx. 80g in 40g of water for 10 minutes.
Carefully roast the pine nuts. The pine nuts should be light brown after roasting. Cut the pine nuts very finely with a large knife or rub them with a nut mill. Pick up some of the seeds to decorate the pesto later.
Place all ingredients in a tall container and chop and mix with a blender. Put the pesto in a bowl or in a glass.
In the fridge, the pesto lasts a while (days to weeks) and is therefore a way to preserve bear's garlic.
You can eat wild garlic pesto as sauce with spaghetti, but it also tastes great with potatoes or bread.

10 Effects of food

10.1 Use ingredients: recommendable

Acai powder	Kudzu
Bitter Herb liqueur	Leaf salads (bitter)
Cream 10% coffee cream	Lettuce
Fox nut, gorgon nut, makhana	Lily bulbs
Hibiscus	Mascarpone cheese

10.2 Use ingredients: yes

Adzuki beans
Agar agar (kelp)
Agrimony
Almond
Almond milk
Almond puree
Aloe juice
Amaranth
Amaranth Pops
Anchovy / Sardine
Angelica root
Anise (Common Fennel)
Apple (sour)
Apple (sweet)
Apple puree
Apricot
Apricots
Arrowroot
Artichoke
Asparagus (green or white)
Aubergine
Baking powder
Balm
Bamboo shoots
Banana
Banana (cooking banana)
Banchatee (green tea)
barberry
Barley
Barley flour
Barley grass powder
Barley grouts
Barley malt
Barley not peeled
Basic recipe for a beef soup
Basic recipe for a beef soup (warming)
Basic recipe for a chicken soup (warming)
Basic recipe for a duck soup
Basic recipe for a fish soup
Basic recipe for a rice soup (Congee)
Basic recipe for a vegetable soup (nutritious)
Basil
Basil (fresh)
Batavia
Bay leaf
Bean oil
Beans (green, fresh)
Bearberry leaf
Beef bone marrow

Beef fillet
Beef heart
Beef heart (calf)
Beef lungs (calf)
Beef meat
Beef meat (calf)
Beef meatbones
Beef Oxtail pieces
Beef soup meat
Beef stomach
Berries of the season
Bitter orange peel
Black beans
Black caraway
Black fungus mushroom
Black tea
Blackberry dried (unripe fruit)
Blackberry leaves
Blackberry's
Black-eyed peas
Blackthorn (Sloe)
Blue mallow tee
Blueberry
Blueberry dried
Bocksdorn fruits (Fructus Lycii, Goji, goji berry dried
Boletus mushroom
Borage
Borage oil
Boxhorn clover seeds
Brazil nuts
Bread with carob kernel flour
Breadcrumbs (wheat bread, bread roll)
Brie cheese
Broad beans (thick beans)
Broccoli
Brussels sprouts
Buckbean
Buckwheat
Buckwheat (roasted) Kasha
Buckwheat whole grain
Bulgur (cereals)
Burdock root tea
Bush beans
Butter (half fat)
Butter beans white
Buttermilk
Calamari
Camembert
Cantaloupe
Capers in olive oil

Carambola (Star fruit)
Cardamom
Carob flour, St. john's bread
Carp
Carrot
Carrot (Early Carrot)
Carrot juice without sugar
Cashews
Cauliflower
Caviar
Celery root
Celery sticks
Cereal coffee
Chamomile
Chamomile tea
Champignon
Channa-Dal
Chanterelle
Chard
Chenpi (Chinese tangerine bowl)
Cherry
Cherry (sour)
Cherry compote
Chervil
Chervil dried
Chestnut puree
Chestnuts
Chicken Blood
Chicken egg
Chicken egg white
Chicken heart
Chicken meat
Chicken stomach
Chicken yolk
Chickpeas
Chickweed
Chicory
Chili (pod or ground)
Chinese cabbage
Chinese pearl barley
Chives
Chlorella (fresh water)
Chrysanthemum blossom tea
Cinnamon ground
Cinnamon sticks
Clementine
Clementines
Clove
Cocoa
Coconut flakes
Coconut grated
Coconut meat
Coconut milk
Cod

Codfish
Coffee
Coix (seeds) YiYi Ren
Cola drink (low calorie)
Compote (fruits of the season)
Coriander
Coriander (fresh)
Corn
Corn (fast polenta)
Corn (roasted)
Corn flour
Corn germ oil
Corn Grease (Polenta)
Corn silk tea
Corn starch
Cottage cheese
Couscous
Cow's milk (1.5% fat)
Cow's milk (whole milk 3.5% fat)
Crab
Cranberries
Cranberry
Cranberry
Cranberry juice
Cream sour 10%
Creamer
Cress
Crispbread
Crucian
Cucumber
Cucumber (bitter)
Cucumber (spicy cucumber)
Cumin (Caraway seed)
Curcuma
Curd cheese 20%
Currant (black)
Currant (red)
Currant (white)
Currants (black)
Currants (red)
Curry
Curry paste red
Daisy
Dandelion (young plants)
Dandelion juice
Dandelion roots tea
Dashi
Dates red
Deer meat
Deer meat
Deer's Bones
Deer's kidneys
Dill
Duck (heart)

Duck (slaughtered)
Ducks egg
Dulse (seaweed)
Dyer's broom herb
Edam cheese
Elderberries
Elderberry blossom tee
Emmental cheese
Endive salad
Evening primrose oil
Fennel
Fennel seeds ground
Fennel tea
Fenugreek (Trigonella foenum-graecum)
Feta cheese
Feta cheese
Fig
Fish innards
Fish pieces mixed (fresh water)
Fish remains
Fish sauce
Flounder
Flower pollen
French beans
Fresh cheese
Fresh cheese from soya
Fresh cheese with herbs
Freshwater crab
Freshwater fish
Fruit tea
Gail plum
Galangal
Garam Masala powder
Garlic
Gelatin white
Gentian root
Gentian root tea
Ginger fresh
Ginger oil
Ginger powder
Ginkgo fruit
Ginseng
Ginseng root
Goat
Goat and sheep's blood
Goat and sheep's brain
Goat and sheep's milk
Goat and sheep's stomach
Goat cheese
Goose egg
Gooseberry
Goose blood
Gouda cheese

Gourd
Grape juice red
Grape juice white
Grapefruit (Pomelo)
Grapefruit dried peel
Grapefruit juice
Grapeseed oil
Grass carp
Green spelt
Green tea
Greengage
Ground
Ground caraway
Guava
Halibut (Flatfish)
Hawthorn
Hazelnuts
Herbal tea mix
Herbs bitter
Herbs of Provence
Herbs various
Herbs wild
Herring
Hibiscus tea
Hijiki
Hokkaido pumpkin
Hop
Horehound leaves
Horse meat
Hyssop
Iceberg lettuce
Jasmine blossoms tee
Jellyfish
Juniper berry
Kaki plum
Kalmus
Kefir
Kidney beans (red)
King Solomon's-seal
Kiwi
Kohlrabi
Kombu seaweed (Saccharina japonica)
Kukicha tea
Kumquats
Lamb bones
Lamb meat
Lamb shoulder
Lamb's lettuce
Lamb's lettuce
Lavender blossoms
Leek
Lemon
Lemon Balm (dried)
Lemon Balm (fresh)

Lemon juice
Lemon peel
Lemongrass
Lentils
Lentils black
Lentils red
Lentils yellow
Licorice root tea
Lima beans
Lime
Lime blossom tea
Linseed
Linseed (crushed)
Linseed oil
Liver smoothing tea
Lobster
Longane
Loquate / Japanese medlar
Lotus roots
Lotus seeds
Lovage
Lovage seeds
Luo Han Guo fruit
Lychee
Lychee in Preserved
Lye roll
Mackerel
Mallow (Malva sylvestris) blossom tea
Malt
Mango
Manioc flour
Maple syrup
Mare's milk
Marjoram
Mediterranean fish (cod, plaice,
haddock, sea eel, mackerel)
Medlar
Millet
Millet flakes
Mineral water
Mirabelle plum
Miso
Miso black (fermented)
Miso paste (soy bean paste)
Mixed Pickles
Mold cheese
Morel (black, dried)
Morel, dried
Mozzarella
Mu Erh Mushroom
Muesli
Mulberry fruit
Mulled Wine Spice
Mullet

Multi-grain bread (gray bread)
Mung bean
Mung bean sprouting
Mussels
Mustard
Mustard Dijon
Mustard medium hot
Mustard seeds
Mustard sweet
Mutton
Mutton
Nasturtium (nose-twister or nose-
tweaker)
Nectarine
Nettles
Noodles (wheat) with egg
Noodles (wheat, lasagne) with egg
Noodles (wheat, ribbon noodles) with
egg
Noodles (wheat, spaghetti) with egg
Noodles (whole grain) with egg
Nori, purple seaweed, red algae
Nutmeg
Oat
Oat flakes (whole grain)
Oat flakes roasted
Oat flour
Oat fusion (baby food)
Oat meal
Oat milk
Octopus
Octopus
Okra
Olive oil
Olives
Olives green
Onion (shallot)
Onion (spring onion)
Onion read
Onion white
Orange
Orange blossom
Orange dried peel
Orange grated peel
Orange peel
Oregano dried
Oregano fresh
Oyster mushroom
Oyster shell powder
Palm oil
Papaya
Parsley
Parsley root
Parsnip

Passion blossoms tea
Passion fruit
Peaches
Peaches (canned)
Peanut oil
Peanuts
Pear
Pearl barley
Pearl barley
Peas
Peas, green
Pepper (ground)
Pepper Cayenne
Pepper powder (hot)
Pepper white (ground)
Peppercorns
Peppermint
Peppermint tea
Pepperoni
Pepperoni, red, pitted, halved
Pepperoni, yellow, pitted, halved
Peppers
Peppers (rose peppers)
Peppers (sweet)
Peppers powder
Perch
Pheasant
Pickle
Pig blood
Pigeon
Pigeon egg
Pimento
Pine nuts
Pineapple
Pineapple (from a can)
Pineapple juice without sugar
Pinto beans speckled
Pistachios
Plaice
Plum
Plum dried
Plums
Pomegranate
Poppy
Pork Bacon
Pork brain
Pork ham
Pork ham cooked
Pork ham smoked
Pork heart
Pork knuckle
Pork lung
Pork marrow bones
Pork meat

Pork skin
Pork stomach
Pork's intestine
Potato
Potato (mealy)
Potato flour
Prickly pear
Processed cheese 12%
Psyllium seed
Pudding powder vanilla
Pumpernickel (dark bread)
Pumpkin
Pumpkin seed oil
Pumpkin seeds
Quail
Quail egg
Quince
Quinoa
Rabbit
Rabbit (wild)
Rabbit meat
Radicchio
Radish
Radish (white, green, purple-red)
Radish black
Radish horseradish
Radish leaves
Rapeseed oil
Raspberry
Raspberry dried (immature)
Raspberry leaf tea
Red beet
Red berry (without sugar)
Red cabbage
Reishi mushroom
Rhubarb
Ribworttea
Rice (fragrance)
Rice (Gaoliang / Sorghum)
Rice (whole grain)
Rice Basmati
Rice black
Rice flour
Rice long grain rice
Rice malt
Rice mash
Rice noodles
Rice red
Rice round grain
Rice starch
Rice sticky
Rice sweet
Rice variety any
Rice wild (nature rice)

Romaine lettuce / lettuce salad
Rose blossom tea
Rose hip
Rose hip tea
Rose leaf tea
Rosefish
Rosemary
Rucola
Rusk
Rye
Rye flour
Rye wholemeal bread
Safflower (Dyer's thistle / Hong Hua)
Saffron
Sage
Sago (cereals)
Sake
Salmon
Salsify
Sauerkraut (cutted cabbage fermented)
Savory
Savoy cabbage / kale
Sea buckthorn
Sea cucumber
Seacrab
Sesame oil
Sesame oil roasted
Sesame paste (Tahini)
Sesame, black
Sesame, white
Shark
Sheep's milk
Sheep's milk yoghurt
Shiitake, dried
Shrimp
Shrimps
Skim milk powder
Slug
Sorrel
Sour cherries
Sour milk
Sour milk cheese 20%
Sourdough
Soy flour
Soy noodles
Soy sauce
Soy Tofu
Soy Tofu smoked
Soya Cuisine (soy cream)
Soybean milk
Soybean oil
Soybeans
Soybeans, black
Soybeans, blacks, fermented

Soybeans, yellow
Spelled (Dark) bread
Spelled flakes
Spelled grain
Spelled semolina
Spelled wholemeal flour
Spinach
Spiny lobsters
Spurdog (spiny dogfish, Schillerlocken)
St. Benedict's thistle, blessed thistle,
holy thistle, spotted thistle
Star anise
Stevia (candyleaf, sweetleaf)
Strawberries
Sugar fructose - fruit sugar
Sugar glucose - grapes sugar
Sugar Milk Sugar
Sugar substitute (sweetener)
Sunflower oil
Sunflower seeds
Sweet potato
Tabasco
Tangerine
Tarragon (Estragon)
Tea mixture uric acid lowering
Thistle oil
Thyme
Thyme dried
Toast bread (whole grain)
Tomato
Tomato dried
Tomato juice
Tomato paste
Tomato puree
Tonic Water
Topinambur
Trout
Trout (smoked)
Truffle
Tsampa (roasted barley flour)
Tuna
Turkey breast meat
Turkey ham
Turmeric (yellow root)
Turnip
Turnips
Umeboshi paste
Umeboshi plums (Japanese apricots)
Valerian
Vanilla
Vanilla pod
Vanilla powder
Vegetable juice
Vinegar (Apple vinegar)

Vinegar (Red wine vinegar)
Vinegar Aceto Balsamico
Vinegar Aceto Balsamico white
Wakame
Walnut oil
Walnuts
Water
Water hot
Watermelon
Wax gourd
Wheat
Wheat bran
Wheat bulgur
Wheat flakes
Wheat flour
Wheat flour whole grain
Wheat germ oil
Wheat semolina
Wheat semolina for children
Wheat/Rye/Gray-black bread with yeast
Wheatgrass juice
Wheatgrass powder

Whey
White beans
White cabbage
Whitefish
Whole grain bread
Wholemeal flour
Wild boar meat
Wild garlic (garlic spinach)
Wild herbs
Wild strawberries
Wormwood herb
Yam root, yam root tuber
Yarrow
Yarrow tea
Yeast
Yew nut
Yoghurt vanilla
Yogi tea
Yogurt (natural, 1.5% fat)
Yogurt (natural, 3.5% fat)
Zucchini

10.3 Use ingredients: little

Acerola fruit nectar or powder
Agave nectar
Almond marzipan
Apple juice (natural cloudy)
Apricot dried
Apricot jam
Apricot nectar
Apricots juice
Avocado
Beef kidney
Beef liver
Beer (alcohol-free)
Beer (alcohol-reduced)
Berry juice
Bitter Lemon
Blackberry jam
Blueberry jam
Blueberry juice
Bread roll
Brown ale
Cherry juice
Chicken liver
Chocolate
Chocolate (Diabetic)
Coconut fat
Cranberry jam
Cream (30% fat)
Cream sour 20%

Cream sour 30%
Cream, sweet 30%
Creme fraiche cheese
Curd cheese 40%
Currant jam (black)
Currant jam (red)
Currant juice (black)
Dates dried
Eel
Eel smoked
Fernet Branca (herbal bitter liqueur)
Fig dried
Fructose (glucose)
Fruit mix juice
Ginseng liqueur
Goat and sheep's liver
Goose
Goose fat
Goose parts
Gorgonzola
Grapes red
Grapes white
Honey
Honey wine (Met)
Ladyfingers
Lamb kidneys
Lamb liver
Lychee liqueur

Mango juice
Margarine
Margarine (diet)
Martini
Mayonnaise 50%
Mayonnaise 80%
Orange jam
Orange juice
Parmesan
Peanut (roasted)
Pear juice
Pork fat (lard)
Pork kidneys
Pork Lard
Pork liver
processed cheese 30%
Prosecco
Rabbit liver
Raisins
Raspberry jam
Red wine
Rum
Salt
Salt (herbal)
Sherry (whine)

Sour cream 15% fat
Spirit
Strawberry jam
Strawberry Juice
Sugar - icing sugar
Sugar brown
Sugar candy white
Sugar cane sugar
Sugar molasses
Sugar palm sugar
Sugar white
Vanilla sugar natural
Walnuts roasted
Wheat beer
Wheat flatbread/pita bread
White bread (baguette)
White bread (pretzel sticks)
White bread (roll)
White bread (wheat bread)
White breadcrumbs
White dumpling bread (wheat bread cut into chunks)
White wine
Wormwood

10.4 Do not use contra-acting foods

Beer (Pils)
Beer (Top-fermented German dark beer)
Bitter liqueur
Butter Bio
Campari
Clarified butter
Cola drink

Cooking oil
Oysters
Peanut butter
Pork sausage (Bratwurst)
Pork/beef sausage (smoked)
Puff pastry
Supplementary nutrition

11 Complementary

11.1 Arnica (wolf's bane)

Arnica montana, flor.
Preparation: Oil for massage
Arnica massage oil promotes blood circulation, loosens the muscles and protects against unpleasant muscle soreness. Massage oil from 10g Arnika flowers and 50g aloe vera oil and let it stand for 3 weeks (possibly put in the sun and shake occasionally).
Dosage: Prepare massage oil from 10g arnica blossoms and 50g aloe vera oil and leave to stand for 3 weeks (if necessary put in the sun and

shake occasionally).

Arnica blossoms are used in: tissue and organ damage (e.g., mechanical effects and disorders of the blood supply); Injuries such as strains, bruises. After washing, bathing, showering or swimming, massage gently into the still moist skin. During pregnancy use regularly to avoid stretch marks.

Notice: It is not recommended to use arnica internally. It can cause nausea, vomiting and heart problems.

11.2 Bath with lavender

Preparation: Healing bath

Calming, regenerates the central nervous system, restlessness, difficulty falling asleep, loss of appetite and nervous bowel problems.

Dosage: Soak in the bath and put a tied bag with the lavender in the water and let it soak for 10 minutes. The bag can be squeezed several times before removing it.

11.3 candyleaf, sweetleaf, sugarleaf

Stevia rebaudiana

Preparation: Cooking addition

Sweetener for diabetics or for weight loss. Hypotensive, antimicrobial, vasodilator effect.

Attention - consult with your doctor or therapist.

Dosage: As sweetener, dried or fresh

Some studies have described teratogenic and mutagenic effects in hamsters and rats, as well as mutagenicity in vitro. Not authorized in the EU as food. Stevia supporters see behind it a conspiracy of sugar lobby and bias of the European Commission. Finally, stevioside has been used in Asia for decades as a sweetener - so far without negative consequences.

Notice: The WHO studies on the effects of steviol in vivo have not shown any evidence of mutagenic effects in humans. Only at your own risk.

11.4 Passion flowers

Passiflora

Preparation: Healing tea (infusion)

Calming, antispasmodic and anxiolytic.

Dosage: Pour cup of freshly cooked water.

Cover the cup well and let it soak for 5 to 10 minutes.

To taste with sugar, honey or sweet candy.

In order to preserve the essential oils, the container should be well

covered.
The daily dose is up to 2 cups. On a cup comes a teaspoon (2-3 g) of dried passionflower.
Notice: Also against sleep disorders.

11.5 Sage root

Salvia miltorrhiza, rad.
Preparation: Different effects
Good against coronary circulatory disorders, post-treatment of heart attack, restlessness and sleep disorders.
Dosage: Notice: Do not use in pregnancy.

11.6 Shepherd's purse

Capsella, Herba Bursae pastoris, herb.
Preparation: Healing tea (infusion)
Reduces uterine bleeding, digestive tract, stool, hemorrhoids, hypertension.

11.7 Valerian

Valeriana
Preparation: Healing tea (infusion)
Lowers blood pressure, tranquilizer, antispasmodic, relief of climacteric symptoms.
Dosage: Pour 2 teaspoons of the tea into 250 ml of boiling water and leave for 10 minutes. Then sieve. Drink 2 to 3 cups per day as needed.
Active ingredients: valeric acid, valepotriate, bicyclic sesquiterpenes, alkaloids

12 Basics of Nutrition

The basic principles of nutrition described herein are general recommendations. They are not aimed at a specific form of therapy. Recommendations concerning a therapy have priority.

12.1 Nutrition

Regular meals in a relaxed atmosphere. A warm breakfast is considered a good start into the day.
The main meals ought to be taken for lunch – supper in the early evening. Pay attention to feeling hungry or sated: don't eat too much nor remain hungry is the rule
Prepare the meals freshly from natural, regional products. Frozen, heat-conserved, industrially prepared or foodstuffs cooked in the microwave oven are rejected.
Choice of foodstuffs according to the season: more cooling food in summer, more warming food in winter.
Eat cooked food at least twice a day. Food and drinks ought to be lukewarm, never ice-cold or hot.
Raw vegetables, briefly cooked vegetables, freshly squeezed juices and mineral water are not recommended. Milk and dairy products are only included in the diet if they don't cause problems.
Don't use therapeutic recipes over a longer period without consulting your doctor or therapist.

Varied food
Enjoy the diversity of foodstuffs. Characteristics of a balanced nutrition are variety, suitable combination and a balanced quantity of rich and low energy foodstuffs (on one hand avoiding undersupply with essential nutrients and on the other hand to take to many undesirable substances).

A lot of Cereal Products - and Potatoes
Bread, pasta, rice, cereal flakes (best wholemeal) as well as potatoes contain almost no fat, but many vitamins, mineral nutrients, trace elements, roughage and secondary plant substances. These foodstuffs ought to be taken with low-fat side dishes.

Vegetables and Fruit – „Take Five" every day …
5 portions of vegetables and fruit a day, as fresh as possible, briefly cooked, or maybe one portion as a juice – ideal as a side dish to every meal as well as snack between meals: Thus a lot of vitamins, mineral nutrients as well as roughage and secondary plant substances

Daily milk and dairy products
Milk and Dairy Products every Day, once or twice per Week Fish; meat, sausages as well as eggs moderately. These foodstuffs contain valuable nutrients like calcium in the milk, iodine selenium and omega-3 fat acids in saltwater fish. Meat is favorable due to its high content of disposable iron and the vitamins B1, B6 and B12. Quantities of 300 – 600 g meat and sausage per week are sufficient. Prefer low-fat products, especially in meat- and dairy products.

Low-fat and fatty Foodstuffs
Fat supplies us with essential fat acids and fatty foodstuffs contain also fat-soluble vitamins. Fat is high in energy; therefore much fat in the food may cause overweight, possibly also cancer. Too many saturated fat acids may further a tendency for cardio-vascular diseases in the long term. Prefer vegetable oils and fats (e.g. rapeseed-, olive-, soya-oils and solid fats produced therefrom). Beware of invisible fat in meat- and dairy products, pastry and sweets as well as in fast-food and convenience foods. 70 – 90 g fat per day is sufficient.

Moderately Sugar and Salt
Take sugar and foods/drinks containing various kinds of sugar (e.g. glucose syrup) only occasionally. Use herbs and spices as well as a little salt creatively. Prefer salt containing iodine.

Plenty of Liquids
Water is absolutely essential. Drink 1-2 l liquids every day. Prefer water (with or without gas) and other low-calorie drinks. Alcoholic drinks should not be taken.

Tasty Dishes, carefully cooked
Cook the meals with as low temperatures and as short as possible, using little water and fat – this preserves the original taste, keeps the nutrients intact and prevents the production of harmful compounds.

Take time and enjoy the food
Take your Time and enjoy your Food
Eating consciously helps to eat right. The eye enjoys food, too. It's fun, invites to enjoy varied dishes and stimulates the feeling of satiety.

Watch your Weight and stay in Motion
A balanced diet and a lot of exercise and sport (30 – 60 min/day) are a healthy combination. The right weight furthers well-being and health. Thermals, directional effectiveness, digestive power

There are various criteria for judging the effectiveness of herbs and foodstuffs.

The use of certain herbs and ingredients is based on observations of the effects on the body which these foodstuffs, herbs and spices show after having eaten them. The medical science has developed following system: Every ingredient or herb has a directional effectiveness. Furthermore, there are herbs which have a special effect on certain organs.

The basic condition for a healthy metabolism is to obtain sufficient energy from food and that the digestive process doesn't use too much energy. An easily digestible meal makes content and sated, doesn't cause flatulence and fatigue after the meal. The perfect spices increase the healthiness of our meals. Very often, just small doses of herbs and spices will suffice. They are not used to make us sated, but to help our digestive organs to digest the food.

12.2 Recipes

The recipes list the ingredients to be used and the cooking instructions show how the dish is prepared. The list of ingredients shows the concerned quantities as well as the relevance for the therapy. If you find „less than mentioned", try to comply or find an alternative from the „list of recommended foodstuffs". Mostly it shall result just in a small change of taste when you simply avoid this ingredient.

Mild cooking methods: boiling, stewing, poaching, steaming
Strong cooking methods: barbecuing, roasting, frying, smoking
Balanced cooking methods: deep-frying, baking brick
Deep-freezing and warming in the microwave oven should be avoided (denaturalization).

12.3 Foodstuffs

Foodstuffs have an effect on body and soul like medicinal herbs, only a very much milder one. Dietary advice is mainly based on regional foodstuffs. The knowledge about the effects of each foodstuff and the knowledge, when which foodstuff shall be used, is based on the orthodox school of medicine. Use ecologic-organic products, if possible. As everything should be cooked for a long time due to a better digestibility and very rarely eaten raw, the food agrees with everyone.

The classification of the foodstuffs according to their effect on the body is the basis in order to achieve a harmonious status of health.

Dietary advisors do not recommend certain foodstuffs for everyone. The individual diet is tailor-made for the individual constitution.

Buy only fresh and ripe fruit and vegetables. You ought to leave unripe fruit and vegetables and such with brown spots and wilted leaves behind in the market. In this case take deep-frozen goods (never ready-to-serve dishes!). Fruit and vegetables are deep-frozen immediately after harvesting and often contain more vitamins and minerals than the goods from the vegetable shelf. Whereas conserved or tinned goods contain very much less biological substances. Also, salt, sugar and others are mostly added to the latter. Never leave the foodstuffs in the water after washing them to avoid that many vital substances get drowned. Clean salads, fruit and vegetables immediately before serving.

Please make sure of the hygienic processing of foodstuffs. Clean your salads, fruit and vegetables carefully. When cooking with meat, prepare all ingredients first and then process the meat products. Clean the worktop and tools very carefully. Wooden surfaces ought to be treated with a mild disinfectant regularly in order to reduce germination.

Store fruit and vegetables separately, if possible. Harvested fruit and vegetables are still alive and emit e.g. ethylene gas, which makes other products ripen and age faster. Keep meat and fish in the closed packaging or store them in the fridge in closed containers.

12.4 Herbs

There are some basic rules for storing medicinal herbs. On principle, herbs must be protected from direct sunlight, humidity and heat.

Containers for the storage of herbs may be glasses, ceramic jars and even plastic containers. However, plastic is a rather unsuitable material and should only be a short-term solution. In case of glass containers, use a dark material.

Medicinal herbs cannot be kept for any long period. The shelf life of herbs is limited. However, it can be prolonged with suitable storage. The place should be dark, rather cool and absolutely dry. A wooden medicine cabinet, placed not directly next to a source of heat, would be ideal. Never buy large quantities of herbs so as not to have to throw them away. Label the container with the name of the herb and the date of harvesting or processing.

13 Other dietic-books

The following syndromes of dietetics, TCM or for a therapy supplement for cancer are available.

Dietetics

E001. Nutrition of the infant - baby food
E002. Nutrition during lactation
E003. Nutrition in old age
E004. Nutrition of children and adolescents
E005. Nutrition of athletes
E006. Light weight
E007. Pregnancy
E008. Full food

Protein and electrolyte - kidneys
E009. (hemodialysis) dialysis treatment
E010. Acute renal failure
E011. Chronic renal insufficiency
E012. Nephrotic syndrome
E013. Kidney stones (nephrolithiasis)

Gastrointestinal tract - pancreas
E014. Acute pancreatitis (inflammation of the pancreas)
E015. Chronic pancreatitis (inflammation of the pancreas)

Gastrointestinal tract - small intestine and large intestine
E016. Acute obstipation (constipation)
E017. Chronic obstipation (constipation)
E018. Colon irritabile
E019. Diverticulitis
E020. Acquired lactose intolerance (lactose malabsorption)
E021. Fructose malabsorption
E022. Glutensensitive enteropathy (celiac disease)
E023. Colectomy
E024. Short Bowel Syndrome

Gastrointestinal tract - liver, gallbladder, bile ducts
E025. Acute and chronic hepatitis (inflammation of the liver)
E026. Cholelithiasis (bile stones)
E027. fatty liver
E028. cirrhosis

Gastrointestinal tract - Stomach and duodenal intestine
E029. Acute gastritis
E030. Chronic gastritis
E031. Stomach bleeding
E032. Ulcus ventriculi and duodenal ulcer
E033. Condition after gastric surgery

Gastrointestinal tract - oral cavity and esophagus
E034. Stomatitis
E035. Esophageal carcinoma (esophageal cancer)
E036. Refluosophagitis (heartburn)

Special diseases
E037. Phenylketonuria (PKU)
E038. Rheumatic joint diseases

Metabolism
E039. Obesity (overweight)
E040. Diabetes mellitus
E041. Eating disorders (underweight)

Fat metabolism
E042. Hypercholesterolaemia (increased cholesterol level)
E043. Hepatic Encephalopathy

Heart and circulation
E044. Arteriosclerosis (arterial calcification)
E045. Heart insufficiency
E046. Hypertension
E047. Hyperuricaemia and gout

Changed nutrient requirements
E048. In case of fever
E049. For malignant diseases
E050. After burns
E051. Radiation and chemotherapy

CANCER
E100. Pancreatic cancer
E101. Bladder cancer
E102. Blood cancer (leukemia)
E103. Breast cancer
E104. Colorectal cancer
E105. Gastric cancer
E106. Kidney cancer
E107. Esophageal cancer

TCM
E200. Bladder - moisture heat in the bladder
E201. Bladder - moisture and cold in the bladder
E202. Bladder - emptiness and cold in the bladder
E203. Large intestine - external cold affects the large intestine
E204. Large intestine - moisture heat in the large intestine
E205. Large intestine - heat blocks the intestine II acute
E206. Large intestine - dryness of the colon
E207. Large intestine - Yang deficiency (cold)
E208. Heart - Blood insufficiency
E209. Heart - Blood stagnation
E210. Heart - Fire
E211. Heart - Hot mucus clogs the heart pores

E212. Heart - Cold mucus clogs the heart pores
E213. Heart - Qi deficiency
E214. Heart - Yang deficiency
E215. Heart - Yin deficiency
E216. Liver - Ascending Liver Yang
E217. Liver - Blood deficiency
E218. Liver - Blood stagnation
E219. Liver - Moisture heat in liver and gall bladder
E220. Liver - Fire
E221. Liver - Gall bladder Qi-Empty
E222. Liver - Cold in the liver meridian
E223. Liver - Qi stagnation
E224. Liver - Wind
E225. Liver - Wind with ascending liver Yang
E226. Liver - Wind with blood anemic
E227. Liver - Wind with extreme heat
E228. Lung - Qi deficiency
E229. Lung - Mucus-moisture in the lungs
E230. Lung - Mucus-heat in the lungs
E231. Lung - Mucus-cold in the lungs
E232. Lung - Dryness of the lungs
E233. Lung - Wind-heat attacks the lungs
E234. Lung - Wind-cold affects the lungs
E235. Lung - Yin deficiency
E236. Stomach - Bloodstagnation
E237. Stomach - Fire
E238. Stomach - Cold with liquid
E239. Stomach - Nutrition stagnation
E240. Stomach - Qi deficiency
E241. Stomach - Rebellious Qi
E242. Stomach - Yin Emptiness
E243. Spleen - Heat and moisture attack the spleen
E244. Spleen - Coldness and moisture affects the spleen
E245. Spleen - Qi deficiency
E246. Spleen - Qi deficiency + Declining spleen Qi
E247. Spleen - Qi deficiency + spleen does not control the blood
E248. Spleen - Yang deficiency
E249. Kidney - Heart and kidney no longer communicate
E250. Kidney - Jing deficiency
E251. Kidney - Kidneys cannot receive the Qi
E252. Kidney - Qi is not stable
E253. Kidney - Yang deficiency
E254. Kidney - Yin deficiency

For further information visit di-book.com.

14 EBNS - Software for nutritional counseling

The main task of the database is to create personalized nutritional advice for each patient individually. The database was developed for Dietetics and Traditional Chinese Medicine.

The Database supports training and advices in the daily work routine.

The computer program provides lists of recipes, ingredients and herbs, which are given to the client. individually adjustable according to patient's request from whole food to vegetarians (lacto, ovo, ...). For every register there is an information sheet which can be given to the client. All texts can be individually designed.

The syndromes can be combined and result in an intersection of the recommended recipes and ingredients. The automated diagnosis for the TCM enables you to check your experience during the training as well as to confirm your diagnosis in the working day. You select several predefined symptoms and have the program automatically display the relevant syndromes.

How to work with the database:
Select the patient / client, select one or more of the syndromes you diagnosed and print the folder.

You can change all values, create new symptoms or syndromes, develop recipes, change or adapt ingredients and herbs to your findings. In simple client management, all relevant data about the person is stored. You get an overview of the past diagnoses and the development of the course of the disease.

As a consultant you save a lot of time when you print out the recipe, food and herbal lists for the recognized syndromes and give them to the clients. You can use this time for a personal conversation. With the database, dieticians and nutritionists can view the nutrients and trace elements for each recipe and develop recipes for syndromes even with suggested ingredients.

All recipe and grocery lists can also be ordered from me as a combination of several diseases. I wish all readers good luck, health and happiness in life.
More information can be found at www.ebns.at.
Volunteer: www.krebsinfo.at
Josef Miligui